AF606560

YANKEE SUPERLATIVES

Published MCMLXXVII by
YANKEE, INC.
Dublin, New Hampshire

Cover: According to our records, Elmer Bitgood of Voluntown, Connecticut, is the strongest man New England has ever produced. Before his death in 1938, the muscle-bound Bitgood hauled a car uphill, raised 2,400 pounds of stone with his shoulders, and lifted the front end of a freight car off a track.

This book has been prepared by the staff of
YANKEE PRESS
Editor Georgia Orcutt
Designer Robert Orlando

FIRST EDITION

Manufactured in the United States of America
Library of Congress Catalogue Card No. 77-87427
ISBN No. 0-911658-82-3

Contents

Foreword

Yankee Superlatives is a compilation of extraordinary records and facts ranging from the smallest to the largest, the greatest to the worst. It is a book that anyone can turn to for an insight into New England and the people who have made the region their home.

We who have assembled this information believe that New Englanders are unique, and this book furnishes a dynamic account of the substance and spirit of their delightful differences, from the region's earliest beginnings to the present day. We have combed through the pages of *Yankee Magazine,* starting with its first issue, and talked with hundreds of people to arrive at our array of distinctions. Some are world records; others hold true for a much smaller geographic area; all pertain to New England.

In our research, we've discovered that superlatives as an entity are both the glue that binds New England together, and the abrasive that separates one place from another. When a New Englander wins an Olympic medal, the entire region unites to cheer him, but when one town challenges an assertion put forward by another town, the fur flies. So, to be fair, we've included some local superlatives as well as some regional records.

We've also learned how difficult it can be to arrive at a superlative and to assign a distinction to a person, a place, or an event. What really constitutes "oldest" or "first" or "greatest" or "last?" If a house is rebuilt from the oldest timbers and bricks, is it still the oldest house? If a ship sails from one port with a crew from another, which town should rightfully claim her glory? These, and hundreds of other questions, are answered in the following pages as we saw fit. Where we couldn't decide an answer ourselves, we've shown both sides of an issue and urge you to be the judge. Some disputes will rage on forever; others may be resolved in minutes.

Mindful of the frivolous as well as the serious, we present only the records we have found interesting, revealing, and enjoyable. We have sought out both the predictable and the surprising, the historical, the forgotten, the moving, the flavorful, the strange, the tragic, the comic, and the bizarre.

Thus, *Yankee Superlatives* embraces the great deeds that New Englanders have accomplished, and is a portrait of their achievements. The result, we feel, is a better understanding of what makes New England the greatest place on earth.

THE EDITORS

1
Looking Back

Last Monument to Redcoats

The evacuation of the British from Boston on March 17, 1776, is commemorated by an eighty-foot marble tower which stands looking out over Boston Harbor from Dorchester Heights, Massachusetts.

Only Monument to Stamp Act

New England's only monument to the repeal of the Stamp Act is located in Dedham, Massachusetts. A group of men organized by Dr. Nathaniel Ames erected the monument, a formidable granite pedestal, on July 22, 1766.

Highest Monument

The Bennington Battle Monument, a 306-foot stone monolith erected in 1891 to commemorate Bennington's efforts in 1777, is the highest stone battle monument in the world.

Only Monument to a Monument

Teddy Roosevelt presented an oak tree to the town of East Haven, Connecticut, in 1908. The tree was to mark the spot where General Lafayette and his men camped during the Revolutionary War. In 1965 a plaque was to be placed near it explaining the history of the old tree, but which tree? There seemed to be a discrepancy over which oak was indeed the Roosevelt oak. Finally a plaque was placed near a tree, identified to most people's satisfaction. This plaque commemorates the tree which commemorates the spot where General Lafayette camped: a monument to a monument, the only one we could find!

The bee pictured at left can be found atop the library in Pembroke, Massachusetts; it is the only such monument in New England.

Only Monument to Doughnuts

Captain Hanson Crockett Gregory invented the hole in the doughnut in 1847. A plaque, placed at his birthplace in Glen Cove, Rockport, Maine, to commemorate his great invention, measures twelve by fourteen inches in size, and was erected by his friends and relatives on November 2, 1947. The captain found it practical to feed snacks to his crew at the wheel of the ship by making a hole in the middle of the cake, called a doughnut, and fitting it snugly over one of the wheel's spokes. It was in rough and heavy seas one day that the captain made the discovery. He could still eat his favorite fried cake while keeping his hands free to manage the wheel by spearing the middle of the cake with the wheel's spoke.

Only Monument to Ether

The first use of ether in medicine is honored by a plaque which is displayed in the Boston Public Garden. This is the only plaque in New England that commemorates the chemical.

Only Monument to Schoolboys

At the corner of School and Main streets in Ashburnham, Massachusetts, stands, as far as we know, the only monument in the United States honoring schoolboys. "The Schoolboy of 1850" by Bela L. Pratt was presented to the town on October 13, 1913, by Ivers Whitney Adams.

First Monument to Washington

A marble bust in the window of the Old North Church in Boston is considered to be the first monument built to George Washington. The bust, made in 1790 by Christian Gulager, is also considered to be the best likeness of George.

First Flight Memorial

"Here on September 13, 1757, John Childs, who had given public notice of his intention to fly from the steeple of Dr. Cutler's Church, performed it to the satisfaction of many spectators." That's what the plaque says! It hangs just left of the gate in the Old North Church courtyard in Boston, Massachusetts, to commemorate the place where the flight occurred. If this plaque is to be believed (we'd like to believe it) then this must be the first unassisted flight of its kind in New England and in the United States. On display in the Old North Church is the *Boston News-Letter* of 1757, which gives a description of the episode. Apparently "a strangely garbed man" flew not once but three times from the steeple of the Old North Church, the last time discharging two pistols on his way to the ground. Needless to say this "flying around" caused quite a commotion in the street and therefore it was declared that "he is forbid flying any more in town."

Tallest Granite Structure

The Pilgrim Monument in Provincetown, Massachusetts, is the tallest all-granite structure in the United States. It stands 252 feet, seven-and-a-half inches high.

First Marble Quarry

America's first marble quarry was established in the Taconic Mountains in Dorset, Vermont, in 1785. The Tomb of the Unknown Soldier and the tomb of Franklin D. Roosevelt are two of the quarry's famous monuments.

Last Hand Stonecutting Shop

The country's last stonecutting shop to utilize only hand processes is located in Newport, Rhode Island. Founded in 1705 in the same small, colonial building near the wharf where it is located today, the John Stevens Shop has produced such famous stone commemoratives as the wall of John F. Kennedy's grave in Arlington National Cemetery, the dedicational plaque of the Prudential Tower in Boston, stones at the Bank of New York and the Smithsonian Institution, and various markers at schools and colleges.

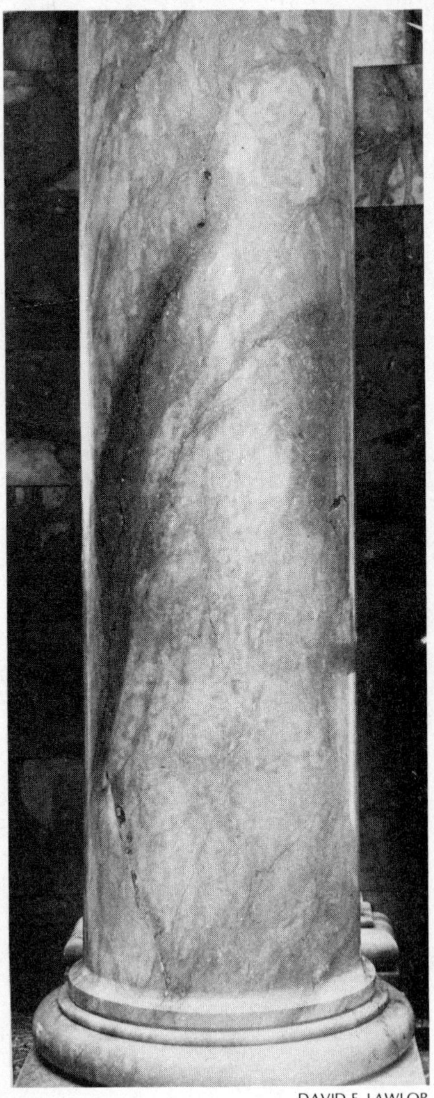

DAVID F. LAWLOR

Most Mysterious Marble

The Bride in White standing in the Hall of Flags of the Massachusetts State House in Boston is visible within the veins of a marble pillar used in the hall's construction. This figure and others, which have appeared, it seems, totally on their own(!), were first observed by Henry G. Weston, a Civil War veteran, who for many years served as a State House guide. We think this is the most unusual, and mysterious marble in New England, and anywhere!

Most Elaborate Mausoleum

Laurel Glen Mausoleum in Cuttingsville, Vermont, was built by John P. Bowman to honor his family. Since he was the last living Bowman at the time the mausoleum was built, he commissioned stonecutters to fashion his likeness kneeling outside the door of the granite and marble edifice holding a wreath and a key. It took 125 sculptors and stonecutters more than a year to complete the Bowman memorial, which was finished in 1881 and contains elaborate marblework, sculpted busts of family members, English Encaustic tile and huge mirrors.

Slowest Stonecutters

It appears that the John Stevens Shop in Newport, Rhode Island, employs the slowest stonecutters in the United States.* They carve, on a good day, three letters an hour! This is because they maintain the artistry of the eighteenth century by using the same methods and tools which were used then.

Only Woman with Face on Abbey

Edith Stedman of Cambridge, Massachusetts, is the only American woman to have her face carved on the wall of an English abbey. She was immortalized in stone at the twelfth-century Norman Abbey in England, a gesture by parishioners and clergy to thank her for her help and dedication in restoring the ancient English church.

Only American in Poet's Corner

Henry Wadsworth Longfellow, England's best-known American poet, is the only American honored with a bust in the Westminster Abbey Poet's Corner. Longfellow was born in 1807 in the old Captain Stephenson house which is still standing in Portland, Maine. Following his death in 1882, he was assigned a place of honor in the famed corner. A subscription was undertaken among his English admirers and on March 2, 1884, Lord Granville made the formal presentation of a marble bust created by Thomas Brock.

**These stonecutters, Mrs. Esther F. Benson, her son John, and two assistants, are considered the best stonecutters in the country.*

First Flag Over Schoolhouse

In 1812, the American flag was raised for the first time over a public schoolhouse. A native fieldstone monument now marks the spot where this occurred on Catamount Hill in Colrain, Massachusetts.

First National Flag

When General Washington took command of the army, he immediately realized the need for a sense of unity among the troops. As it was, each unit marched under its own flag and animosities and jealousies flared among the separate units. Upon Washington's request, the search for a single, national standard began. In six weeks a congressional committee selected a flag — America's first national flag — which was flown for the first time on New Year's Day, 1776, on Prospect Hill in Somerville, Massachusetts. The spot is marked by a granite memorial tower and observatory built by the city in 1902.

First Boston Beacon

A sixty-foot shaft with an eagle on top located on Beacon Hill in Boston marks the spot of the first observation post, or beacon. In 1634, the General Court of Boston decided to place a beacon on the highest hill for protection and as a means of warning the scattered inhabitants of impending danger. If a warning was to be sent from the post, the watchman would climb the pole and light a fire.

Only Liberty Pole Raiser

Until V. Leslie Hebert of Weymouth, Massachusetts, took on the job of liberty pole raising, most of the rituals and customs had been forgotten. The original liberty pole, a symbol of freedom and rebellion at the time of the American Revolution, was used to signal townspeople to meetings. In 1964, Hebert started a campaign to reinstate liberty pole ceremonies. Many towns in what were the original thirteen colonies now reenact the custom annually, and many have employed Hebert as Grand Marshal. When preparations were being made for the Bicentennial he was recognized for what he is — the only professional liberty pole raiser in New England.

PAUL A. DARLING

Only Spite Tower

The only tower we've ever heard of that was constructed just for spite is located in Adamsville, Rhode Island. Built before the turn of the century by Dr. John G. Hathaway when his love was spurned by a local girl, the tower blocked his view of her family's store where she worked.

First Railroad Monument

In the summer of 1826, Quincy quarrymen started blasting granite to build the Bunker Hill Monument. Transportation of huge slabs presented something of a problem, so Gridley Bryant, the man in charge, devised a rail system which is now considered to be the first railway with iron-covered rails in America. The first rails were used to transport the granite from the hills of West Quincy to the Neponset River, two-and-three-quarters miles away. Obelisks with plaques were erected sometime later to commemorate the old roadbed.

Only Gavel from First Railroad

The gavel used at the Massachusetts Republican Convention of 1936 in Springfield, Massachusetts, is the only one of its kind. It was fashioned from a sleeper (a railroad tie) belonging to the first railway at the quarry which supplied the stones for the Bunker Hill Monument.

Oldest Fossil

The oldest fossil ever uncovered in New England, as far as we can tell, is Old Dry Bones, dug out of the Hill-Stead estate in Farmington, Connecticut. First discovered in August, 1913, the skeleton belonged to a giant mastadon that roamed the swamps of the Connecticut Valley between 25,000 and 50,000 years ago.

First Dinosaur Prints

In 1800, when Pliny Moody was plowing a field in South Hadley, Massachusetts, he came across the first dinosaur fossil to be unearthed in New England. Since the slab of rock resembled the footprint of a large bird, Moody assumed that the fossil was a relic of Noah's raven.

Only Mummy Buried in US

No one can say how it got there for sure, but absolutely, positively there are Egyptian mummy ashes buried in Middlebury, Vermont. According to the most rational explanation, Henry L. Sheldon, whose home is now the Sheldon Museum in Middlebury and who was a great collector of odd items, found the mummy in a New York warehouse in 1886. He brought it back to Middlebury and soon set it up in his newly incorporated museum. However, in 1945, long after Sheldon's death, museum trustees decided to send the decaying mummy to the dump. George Mead, a director of the museum, was horrified at the idea and secretly gave the mummy a proper burial, destroying the whole purpose of mummification! Anyway, the headstone can be seen in the cemetery in Middlebury. It reads: Ashes of Amun-Her-Khep-Esh-Ef aged two years, son of Sen Woset third King of Egypt and his wife Hathor-Hotpe, 1883 BC. Mead is buried directly behind the ancient mummy.

Only Elephant Memorial

In Alfred, Maine, a bronze plaque marks the spot where America's first circus elephant was shot and killed by an unknown miscreant. Old Bet was her name and she was touring the "wilds of Maine" with her owner, Hackaleah Bailey, in 1816. A few shots were heard, Old Bet stumbled and fell to the ground. No motive for the slaying was ever uncovered nor was the criminal ever found. On July 24, 1963, the Sanford-Alfred Historical Society, Inc. unveiled the bronze plaque to Old Bet on the spot where she was slain. The plaque was given by the Circus Fans of America. Old Bet is, to our knowledge, the only elephant with a memorial in her honor in New England, as well as the only elephant murdered in cold blood in New England.

Largest Mound of Shells

A mound of oyster shells amounting to an estimated 7,000,000 bushels found along the Damariscotta River in Maine attests to the Indians' apparent love for shellfish. The shells comprise the largest such mound known in New England.

PEABODY MUSEUM OF SALEM

Only God of War

Kukuilimoku, a Hawaiian god of war, one of three such carvings left in the world today, and the only one of its kind in New England, is displayed at the Peabody Museum in Salem, Massachusetts.

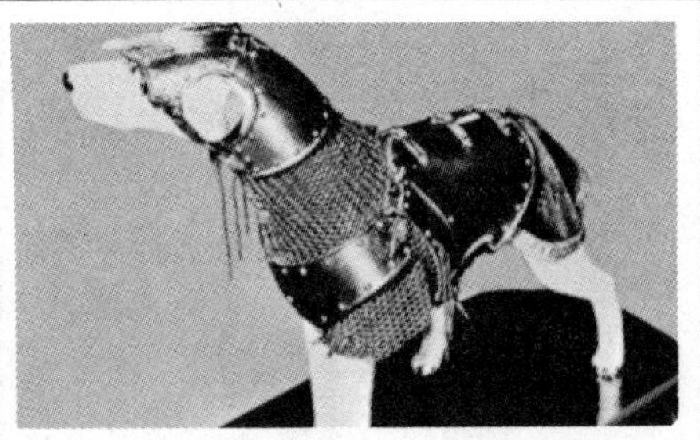

Only Dog Armor

The only known suit of dog armor in New England is on display at the John Woodman Higgins Armory in Worcester, Massachusetts. Made to show the protection placed on prize hunting dogs during the sixteenth century, the suit, crafted from a breastplate of that era, was made by Leonard Heinrich in 1929.

Only Bee on Library

We've seen many different animal forms on weathervanes in our time, but in Pembroke, Massachusetts, we've found what we feel certain is New England's only bee on a library.

And here's how the bee came to be. In the fall of 1974, Madelon Baltzer, assistant librarian at the Pembroke Public Library, discovered that a public spelling bee in May of 1875 had raised the funds for the library's first books. So officials decided to celebrate the library's 100th anniversary by featuring a free spelling bee. During the planning session, Alan Dunphy, a former library trustee, suggested erecting a weathervane in the shape of a bee to adorn the cupola.

Richard Edlund, a Pembroke artist and designer, was asked to design and execute the idea, but he changed the concept to a sculpture in the round. He constructed the bee's skeleton from hundreds of pieces of wood, and bolted it to lightweight, one-inch aluminum tubular legs. Over that he used bronze screening to form the skin, and then applied a weather-tight plastic surface.

The forty-seven-inch high, forty-six-pound bee was mounted upon the cupola's existing lightning rod with the help of the Pembroke Fire Department on the morning of May 10, 1975.

VERMONT DEVELOPMENT DEPARTMENT

Only Monument to First Morgan

Justin Morgan had a horse he appropriately named Justin Morgan, who was born in Randolph, Vermont, in 1789, and died thirty-two years later. This was the first "Morgan Horse." In 1921, 100 years after the horse's death, the Morgan Horse Club of America presented a monument in his honor to the US Department of Agriculture. The monument, which stands on the Morgan Horse Farm in Weybridge, Vermont, is the only such memorial to the first Morgan.

Largest Monument to a Horse

Colonel Redfield Proctor, the Vermont quarry king, built a twenty-two ton marble monument to his Civil War horse "Old Charley." This stone, which has to be the world's largest monument to a horse, is still standing in Proctor.

Most Revered Horses

Daniel Webster loved his horses so much that he insisted on burying them standing up with their shoes on; he also placed Latin epitaphs on their headstones. They were buried at Webster's farm in Marshfield, Massachusetts.

Only Monument to a Chicken

A plaque imbedded in stone in Adamsville, Rhode Island, commemorates the birthplace of the Rhode Island Red breed of fowl. It was built in 1925 by the Rhode Island Red Club of America with the support of Rhode Island Red breeders all over the world on land donated by Deborah T. Manchester. To our knowledge this is the only monument to a chicken in New England.

PAUL A. DARLING

Only Monument to a Titmouse

The tiny tufted titmouse is immortalized in Massachusetts. Some admirer of one of the smallest New England birds erected a monument in Plymouth County to the little feathered fellow. The monument is the only one we know of to a titmouse and is a tombstone, apparently erected in memory of somebody's beloved bird.

First Maypole

In Merrymount, Massachusetts, Thomas Morton erected the first maypole, which first became a symbol of Morton's idolatry, debauchery, and licentious behavior. It later figured into a more innocent celebration of spring.

DICK SMITH

Only Monument to a Cheese

We are certain that the cheese press shown here is the only monument in the world commemorating a real "big cheese." The largest cheese ever made in New England weighed 1,235 pounds and was pressed in Cheshire, Massachusetts* at the farm of Elisha Brown, Jr. It was presented to President Thomas Jefferson in the East Room of the White House in 1802 by Elder John Leland of Cheshire, Massachusetts, who "despite opposition of every other pulpit in Massachusetts carried every vote in Cheshire for the election of President Thomas Jefferson." The monument was erected after the occasion to commemorate Leland, Jefferson, and the cheese — in that order.

**Cheshire farmers established the first cheese factory cooperative in America in 1801, another record for the Massachusetts town.*

Largest Revolving Globe

In twenty brilliant colors the world's largest revolving globe stands outside Coleman Hall at Babson College in Wellesley, Massachusetts. The globe represents the earth as it appears from 5,000 miles out in space. It is twenty-eight feet in diameter, weighs twenty-five tons, and revolves on its axis simulating day into night and the four seasons.

Largest Relief Model of US

Also on the campus of Babson College is the largest relief model of the United States. On December 31, 1940, after fourteen years of interruptions and slowdowns, workmen completed the map which shows the United States as it would look from 700 miles above the earth. Sixty-five feet long and forty-five feet wide, it is topographically correct and greatly detailed.

Largest Steaming Kettle

America's largest steaming kettle is suspended above the sidewalk at the corner of the Sears Crescent building in Boston. The kettle has a capacity of 227 gallons, two quarts, one pint, and three gills. It can be seen actually steaming any season, day or night.

ANASTASI OF BOSTON

First Public Clock

In 1726, the Avery-Bennett Clock was built by two parishioners and became the first "publick" clock in New England. It hangs in the Old North Church and still keeps accurate time.

Most Amazing Watch

Thomas W. Lawson, New England financial wizard and giant of the stock market of the early 1900s, asked Tiffany and Company to make him a watch. It took Edward Koehn, a Swiss watchmaker, a year to make the $10,000 timepiece Lawson requested. Set in the crown of the watch was an Alexandrite, a semi-precious stone which is green by daylight and red by artificial light. The most amazing feature of the watch was its chime mechanism — the watch chimed fifteen minutes before the opening and closing of the stock market. Lawson put great store by his watch — he blamed financial failure and success on it. There was never a watch made like it and there is no one capable of repairing it. That's why a private Boston collector is now the proud possessor of the Lawson watch which no longer chimes or even tells time.

Oldest Organ

The Congregational Church in South Dennis, Massachusetts, houses an organ that is 215 years old and is reputed to be the oldest organ in playing condition in the United States. It was made in 1782 by the great German organ builder, John Snetzler. Where it was originally destined in this country is unknown, but it found a home in South Dennis and it is still played at every Sunday service.

Oldest Revere Bell in Use

For 182 years the belfry of the Congregational Church in Groveland, Massachusetts, has been host to a Revere bell, the oldest still in use. Inscribed with the trademark "Revere 1795," this was the tenth bell cast by Revere himself and is the second oldest Revere bell in existence today. Revere's first bell has been retired in recent years to the auditorium of St. James Episcopal Church in Cambridge, Massachusetts.

First Bells for North America

Old North Church in Boston, Massachusetts, long famous as the church where the lantern signal was hung for Paul Revere, claims to have rung the first bells cast for the British Empire in North America. The bells, arranged to ring in a peal of eight, were cast in 1744 in Gloucestershire, England, and combined they weigh 7,272 pounds. They still ring true, as they did to proclaim the repeal of the Stamp Act, the surrender of Cornwallis, and more recently, the arrival of Gerald Ford and Queen Elizabeth II to the Old North Church for the Bicentennial.

Strongest Door in Deerfield

The only remainder of the first Deerfield settlement, a door complete with tomahawk marks which dates to the leap year 1704, is enclosed in glass at Memorial Hall in Deerfield, Massachusetts. According to what we consider to be fairly reliable reports, the door, built of solid oak with a heavy bolt, was so strong that the attacking Indians were unable to break it down. Frustrated but undaunted, they were forced to use the windows as entrances.

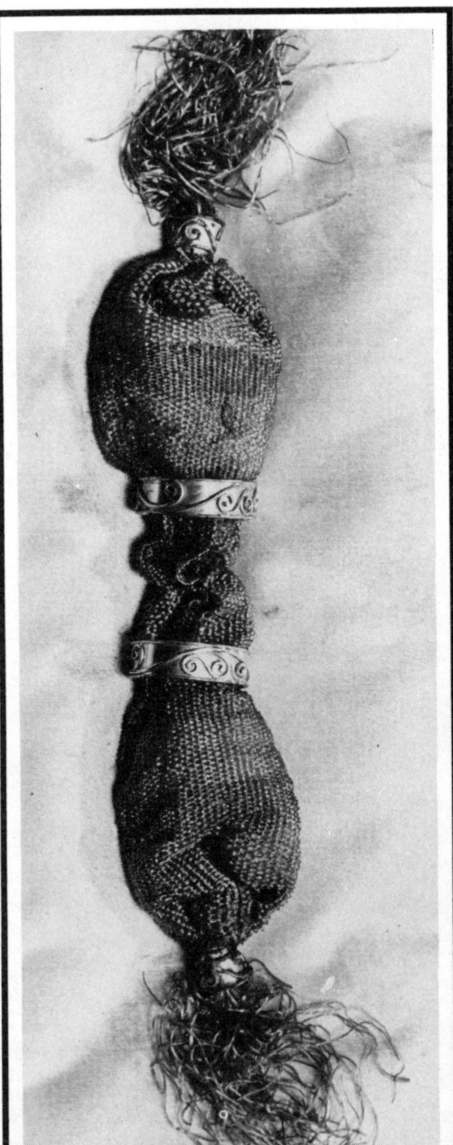

Only Silk Purse from Sow's Ear

It took 200 sows' ears but the Arthur D. Little Company of Cambridge, Massachusetts, accomplished the impossible and made the first (and only) silk purse from a sow's ear. Thousands of experiments were tried — costing thousands of dollars. The company never plans to make another but believes their efforts "have made a contribution to philosophy."

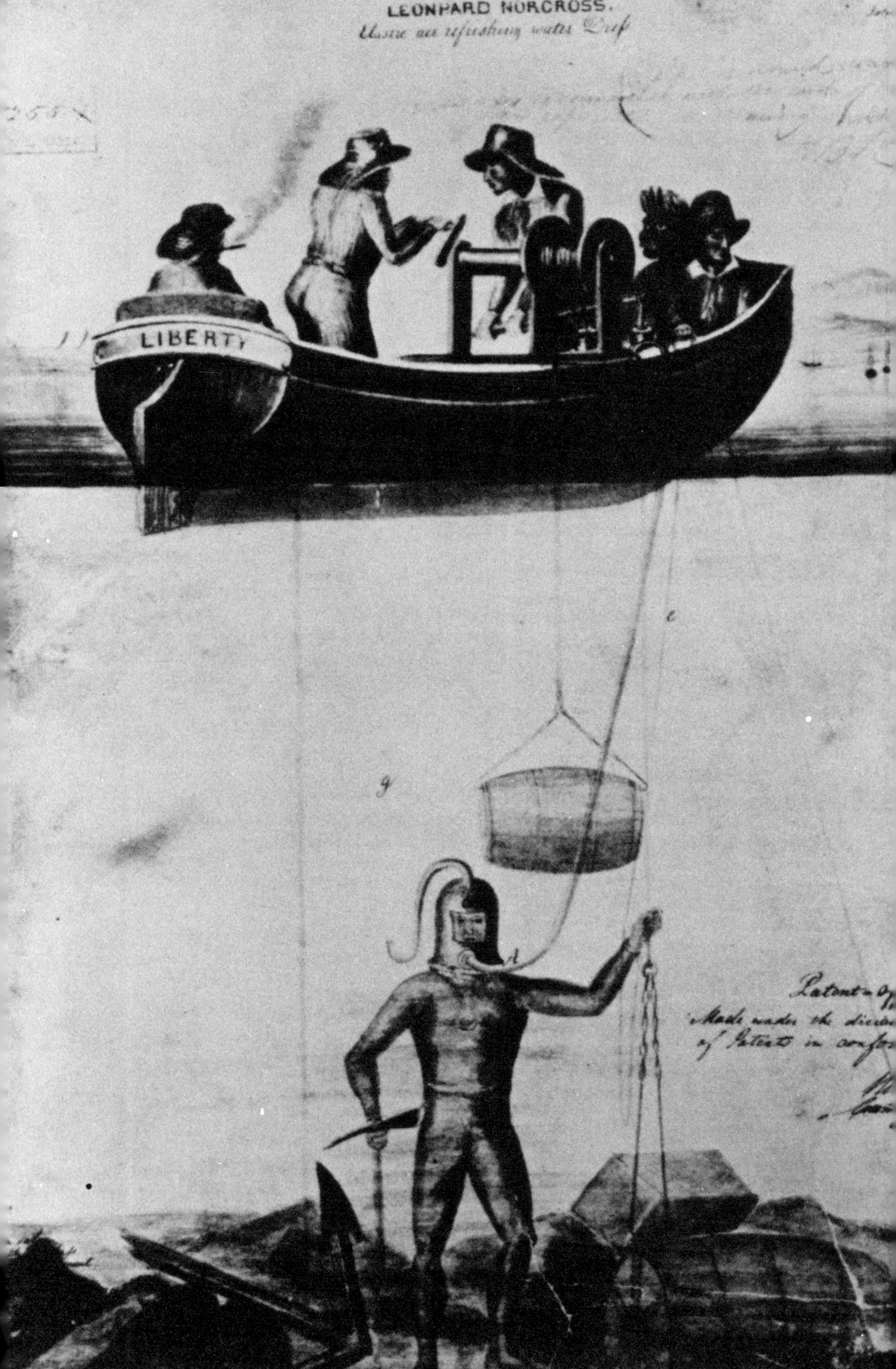
LEONPARD NORCROSS.
LIBERTY

2
Yankee Ingenuity

First Ice-Cream Cones

While visiting the New York World's Fair, E.W. Hobbs of Salem, Massachusetts, saw his first sugar cones. Ice cream, previously only sold in dishes in New England, looked awfully tasty in sugar cones! So, he took the idea back to his little stand, The Willows, at the beach in Salem, and began to make and sell ice-cream cones. This is the first place ice-cream cones were sold in New England. The little stand was also the first place in these parts to sell hot dogs.

First Tollhouse Cookie

When Ruth G. Wakefield opened an inn in a tollhouse on the Boston-to-New Bedford road she made ordinary sugar cookies for her customers. One day, around 1930, she decided to add chocolate chips to sweeten her favorite recipe, and baked America's first tollhouse cookies. During World War II, these cookies rose to even greater fame when mothers and sweethearts mailed millions to overseas soldiers.

First Hamburger

At the grill of Louis's Lunch, a small lunch wagon in New Haven, Connecticut, the hamburger was born. Louis Lassen, Sr., operator of the stand in 1900, created the hamburger by grinding beef trimmings from his famous steak sandwich. He made a patty and grilled it with a thin slice of onion. One day a customer yelled, "Hey Louis, put that hamburger on toast and let me get out of here!"

The illustration at left shows the world's first diving suit, patented by Leonard Norcross of Dixville, Maine, in 1834.

Largest No-Stick Frying Pan

Alcoa Company constructed the world's largest frying pan and Dupont Company covered it with a no-stick Teflon coating. This mammoth pan, kept in Belfast, Maine, measures ten feet and one inch in diameter and can cook 600 eggs at once! (But then Belfast greatly needed a pan this size to feed the thousands of people who come to their annual Egg Festival.)

First Microwave Oven

Waltham, Massachusetts, is the home of the first microwave oven. In 1946, Percy L. Spencer of Raytheon Company prepared food in the first microwave oven and is credited as its inventor.

First Two-Sectioned Lobster Trap

The two-sectioned lobster trap, widely used by lobstermen all over the world was developed in nineteenth-century New England. The "kitchen" holds the bait; the "parlor" is where the lobster waits to be hauled in.

Largest Lobster Pot

Visitors at the annual Rockland, Maine, seafood festival can savor lobsters that have been cooked in the world's largest lobster cooker. The pot cooks four crates of lobsters at once!*

Oldest Eyeglasses

The oldest eyeglasses in New England are preserved in a private collection. Resembling aviator's goggles, the historic glasses were worn by a Pilgrim in the early 1600s in Plymouth, Massachusetts.

**The festival also displays the world's largest lobster trap. It stands about eight feet tall and is approximately sixteen feet long.*

NEW ENGLAND MERCHANTS BANK

First Earmuffs

Chester Greenwood of Farmington, Maine, invented the earmuff at the age of fifteen. While ice-skating in the cold winter of 1873, Chester suffered freezing ears. Disgusted with his plight, he fashioned ear protectors: a wire with fur on either end attached to his hat. It kept his ears warm! On March 13, 1877, he patented the earmuffs (then called earlaps). With further ingenuity he invented a machine to manufacture Greenwood's Champion Ear Protectors and set himself up in a lucrative business.

First Diving Suit

Leonard Norcross of Dixville, Maine, patented the first diving suit in 1834. His "diving armor," made of elastic and metal, was designed to help raise sunken goods from the ocean floor.

Most Famous Hunting Shoe

L.L. Bean, founder of the famous store in Freeport, Maine, first introduced his famous leather and rubber hunting shoe in 1912. Distressed with freezing feet and soggy shoes, he undertook the project of developing the perfect boot: lightweight, waterproof, and warm.

Only Bread Wrapper Hats

We all know of the versatility of plastic bread wrappers, but did you ever hear of wearing them? Miss Marion LeRoy of Winchester, Massachusetts, does. Several years ago a friend gave Miss LeRoy a place mat that was crocheted from strips of plastic cut from bread wrappers. As she studied the artwork and design, she said she decided to try the same technique to make a hat. She cut a few wrappers into one-half-inch strips and after about five hours, (and fifteen wrappers), she produced her first masterpiece, which was a little shaky, she admits, but her expertise improved with each new variety of hat.

After collecting wrappers from her friends, Miss LeRoy cleans them and sorts them into color piles for special blends and designs. She also makes "bread-wrapper" party baskets and place mats, but the popularity of her hats has surpassed her greatest expectations.

"My ninety-four-year-old mother is my best model," LeRoy brags, "because she has that certain knack for wearing these hats." They are lightweight and cool in summer, warm in winter, crush-proof, waterproof, and can be worn for a number of functions — gardening, hanging laundry, social events, and night clubbing. And, if nothing else, they make excellent conversation pieces.

Courtesy of Florence O'Donnell

Oldest Large Chair

Although a number of oversized chairs have been built in New England, the oldest one we could find still standing is located in South Gardner, Massachusetts, in front of Ralph Curcio's chair shop. Built in 1939, the ladderback chair originally stood thirteen feet high and six feet across; but over the years as it has aged, the chair has shrunk and now stands twelve feet, ten-and-three-eighths inches.

Largest Chair

The world's largest chair stands on Elm Street in Gardner, Massachusetts. To commemorate Gardner's place on the map as "Chair City," the local Rotary Club commissioned Leon W. LaPlante of Winchendon, Massachusetts, to build the giant piece of furniture in 1976. LaPlante designed the chair, and in approximately eight-weeks worth of time, he built it to stand twenty feet, seven inches high. It measures eight feet from front to back, and has a depth of ten feet.

STEPHEN T. WHITNEY

First to Own Rocking Chair

Ellis Brewster of Kingston, Massachusetts, is popularly believed to be the first New Englander to own a chair that rocked. Around 1780, Brewster's ancestor, Deacon Brewster, had a farmhand who constructed a cradle-like chair for an invalid in the house.

Most Comfortable Furniture

Scott Dickerson of Brooksville, Maine, makes the most comfortable furniture to be found anywhere in New England. He constructs his custom-made chairs only after taking careful measurements of his client's bodies and adjusting the seats and backs to fit perfectly. In addition to chairs, Dickerson designs tables, spinning wheels, stools, and other furniture.

First Carpenter's Square

In 1817, Silas Hawes, a wheelwright from Vermont, welded two pieces of steel together at right angles and invented the carpenter's square. He took his idea to Stephen Whipple's manufactory in Shaftsbury, Vermont, which had a trip hammer he needed to weld the square.

First Monkey Wrench

Loring Coes of Worcester, Massachusetts, made the first monkey wrench and patented it on April 16, 1841.

NEW ENGLAND MERCHANTS BANK

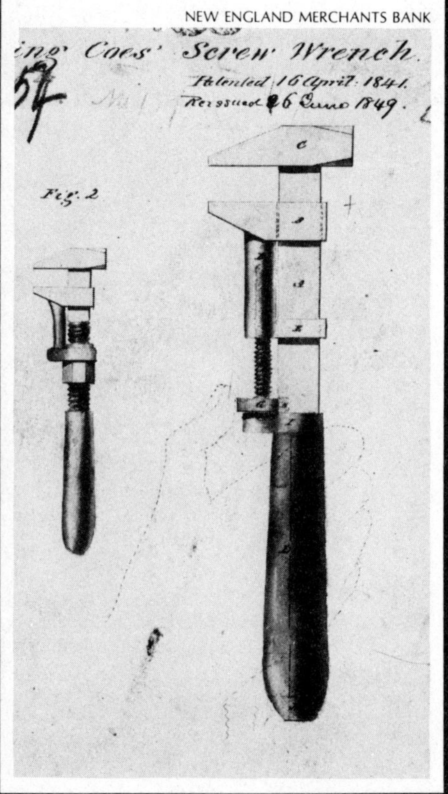

First Felling Ax

New England was the birthplace of America's first felling ax. The tool was designed around 1846 to clear heavily forested countryside.

First Vulcanization of Rubber

After many years of trial and error, Charles Goodyear discovered the process of vulcanizing rubber in Woburn, Massachusetts, in 1839. The process he introduced made rubber withstand extreme temperatures and revolutionized the industry. Ironically, he made the discovery by accident when he dropped rubber treated with sulfur onto a hot stove. He patented the process in 1844, but suffered numerous court injunctions and prosecution from patent-right battles and dishonest business associates. And despite his good ideas, he also spent time in jail for debts he could not pay. Final patent victory occurred in 1852 when Daniel Webster defended him in court. But despite this achievement, a destitute Goodyear died in New York City in 1860 no richer for his discovery.

New Haven Firsts

The Bradley-Smith Company of New Haven was the first to make candy on a stick called the lollipop.

Blotting paper was invented in New Haven by Joseph Parker, who was also the first to manufacture tissue paper.

New Haven-born Frank J. Sprague, who once assisted Thomas Edison, invented the electric elevator.

In 1835, the Blake brothers of New Haven invented mortised locks to replace the popular box lock.

The world's first switchboard opened in New Haven, and was built from wire and pot handles by George W. Coy. The Reverend John E. Todd was the first customer to apply to Coy for service.

Professor A.C. Twining of Yale University invented the first ice-making machine.

In 1851, the first stonecrusher was built by Eli Whitney Blake of New Haven. For this invention he is named "Father of America's Highways."

NEW ENGLAND MERCHANTS BANK

First Platform Scale

In 1831, the first platform scale used to weigh cargo was patented by Thaddeus Fairbanks, a resident of St. Johnsbury, Vermont. The invention, which replaced the time-consuming balance scale, received its patent on June 30, 1831.

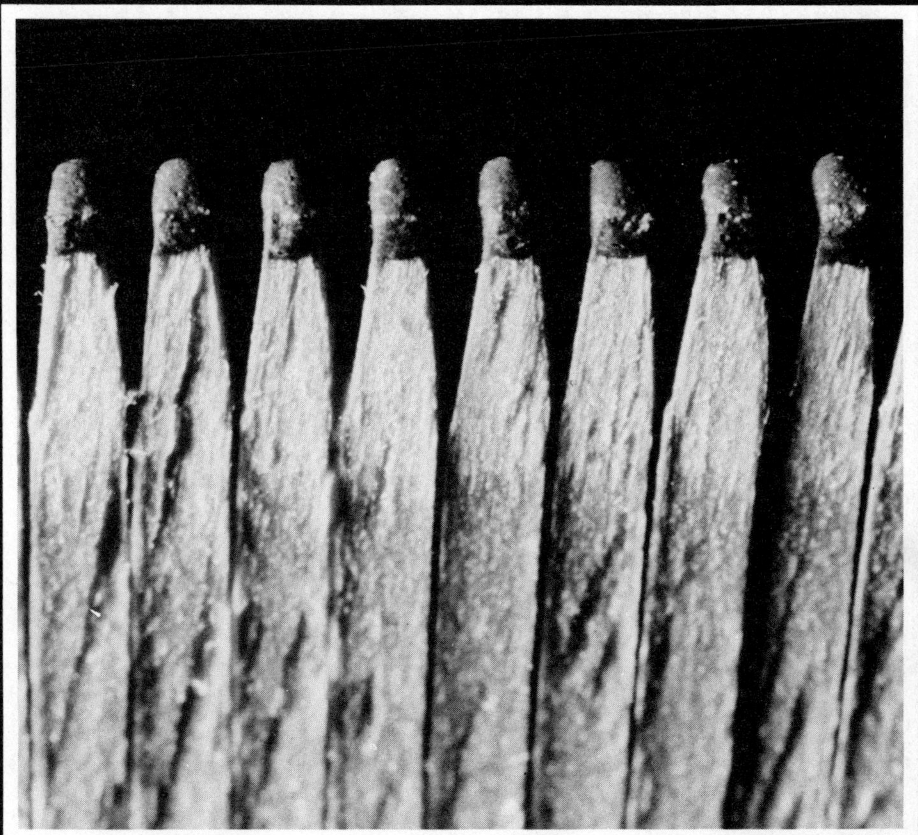

NEW ENGLAND MERCHANTS BANK

First Friction Matches

On October 24, 1836, Alonzo Dwight Phillips of Chicopee, Massachusetts, patented the first friction matches. Considered highly dangerous and inflammable, they were the first practical substitute for flint and steel. Phillips made the matches from a very poisonous process and sold them door-to-door.

First Safety Razor

In the summer of 1895, King C. Gillette came up with a plan for the first safety razor. While working for a cork and seal company and living in Brookline, Massachusetts, he was advised to invent "something that people will use and throw away," thereby developing a continuous market. Standing in front of his bathroom mirror with a dull razor in his hand, Gillette remembered those words and the first safety razor was born. Gillette said that it is one of "the biggest little things ever issued from the US Patent Office." The Gillette Company of Boston was incorporated in 1901.

Largest Safety Razor

Measuring sixteen-and-three-eighths inches in length with an eight-inch blade and weighing a muscle-twitching fourteen pounds of solid brass, the largest razor in the world was made by Gillette of Boston, Massachusetts, as a promotional gimmick. The only one of forty that remains in private hands and in original condition is owned by Alan Dunfey, a Pembroke, Massachusetts, man. All were recalled during World War II to be melted down but only thirty-three were returned. Some were made into lamps and andirons and one, as far as we know, has never been found.

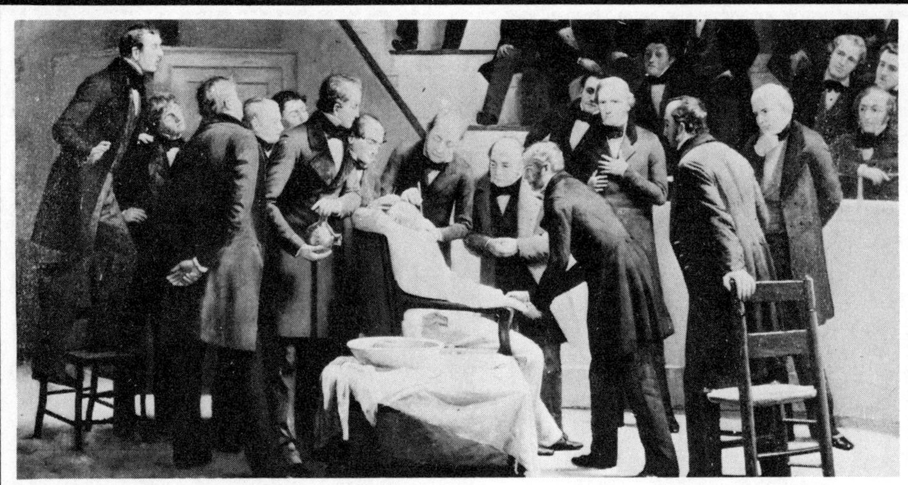

First Use of Anesthesia

Massachusetts General Hospital in Boston was the first place in the world to use surgical anesthesia. The historic event took place when Dr. John Collins Warren removed a tumor from a pioneering patient on October 16, 1846. (William Thomas Green Morton, a dentist, administered ether to the patient.) Afterward, Dr. Collins proudly pronounced, "Gentlemen, this is no humbug."

First Appendectomy

The world's first appendectomy took place at Boston's Massachusetts General Hospital. Prior to 1886, doctors had no cure for the malady, termed "acute inflammation of the bowels." Dr. Reginald H. Fitz first pinpointed the appendix as the culprit and recommended radical surgery.

First Kidney Transplant

In 1950, a team of physicians from Peter Bent Brigham Hospital in Boston, Massachusetts, created the first artificial kidney machine. Subsequently, they are credited with successfully performing the first kidney transplant operation.

Only Fever Named for a City

Streptobacillus monilitormis, a form of rat-bite fever and a deadly strain of bacterium, first appeared on the American scene in 1925 in the Massachusetts city of Haverhill. Thousands died during the outbreak. This fever soon came to be known as Haverhill Fever, and has the dubious distinction of being the only fever or other affliction to be named for an American city.

First Cardiac Pacemaker

Dr. Paul Zoll invented the electric cardiac pacemaker in 1952 at Beth Israel Hospital in Boston, Massachusetts. The device gives constant stimulation to the weak or ailing heart muscle.

First Hospital Social Workers

In 1905, Dr. Richard Cabot established the practice of using trained social workers at bedsides in Massachusetts General Hospital to relieve pressures of mind and spirit and aid therapy and recovery. He was the first to institute this new concept in patient care.

First Mass Innoculation

In 1721, Dr. Zabdiel Boylston directed the first mass innoculation program in Boston, Massachusetts. A handbill circulated to advertise the event welcomed "all sorts of persons, whites, blacks, and of all ages and constitutions" to receive their smallpox medicine.

Oldest Medical School

Harvard's School of Medicine is the oldest medical school in New England, having opened in 1782.

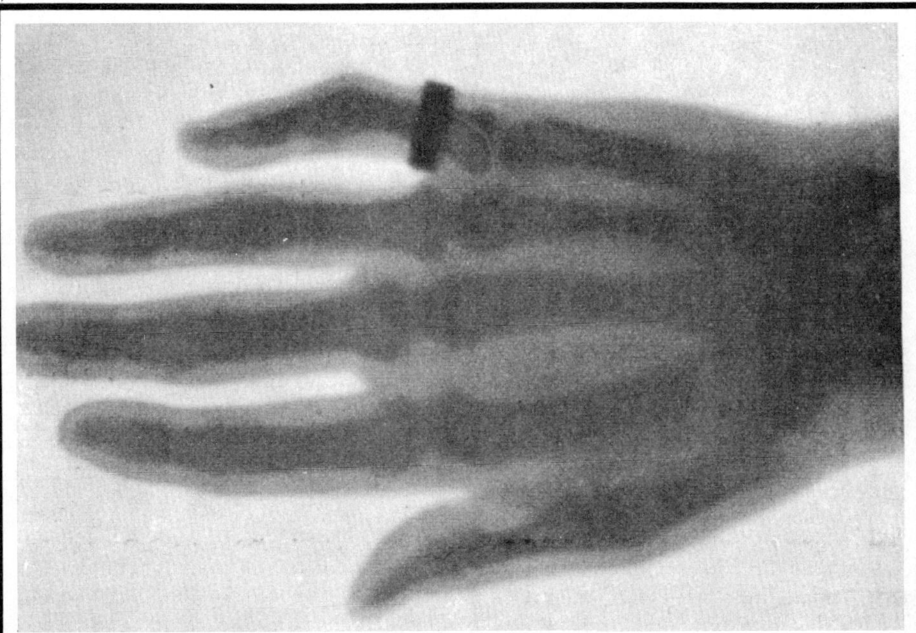

GREAT DEBATE

First X-ray?

Professor Charles Hutchins, head of the Physics Department of Bowdoin College in Brunswick, Maine, supposedly took the first x-ray picture (of Dr. Gilbert M. Elliot's hand) this side of the Atlantic in 1897. At the time, scientists and doctors had no practical medical application for it. According to one source, a man named Perley Watson, a laborer on the Maine Central Railroad, asked Elliot to x-ray his bad back. If this is true, Watson would be credited with giving meaning to the x-ray and making it a valuable medical tool.

But, it's not as simple as that! Dartmouth College in Hanover, New Hampshire, also claims to have taken the first x-ray picture. The procedure, scientifically documented in the Physics Lab of Dartmouth College, took place when a young patient participated in the event by having his injured hand examined by x-ray under the supervision of two brothers, Professor E.B. Frost and Dr. Gilman D. Frost.This x-ray, shown here,took place on February 3, 1896, one year prior to Bowdoin's x-ray picture!

First Movies

The movie-making industry had a formidable forerunner in the stereoscope invented by Cambridge, Massachusetts, resident Oliver Wendell Holmes in 1859. The "scope," which displayed scenes viewed with awe and delight by thousands in parlors all across the country in the late 1800s, was a hand-held viewer which turned two negative pictures into a scene. (As one farmer exclaimed, "It's like you're right there smack dab in the middle!") The pictures were called stereographs and the production of them made the sleepy town of Littleton, New Hampshire, a booming "gay-nineties Hollywood." Littleton became the center of the picture industry when two brothers, Ed and Ben Kilburn, began the production of stereographs and stereoscopes. Many Littleton natives made their movie debut in a four-story building on Cottage Street which became the "studio" and factory for the Kilburn business. The simple pictures were later sold as sets to depict a historical event or to tell slightly risque stories.

SMITHSONIAN INSTITUTION

Sewing Machine Firsts

In 1843, Elias Howe, Jr. built the first practical sewing machine in Boston, Massachusetts. Howe's machine, patented in 1846, included the first eye-pointed needle and shuttle which firmed the stitches.

An earlier New Englander, the Reverend John Adams Dodge of Monkton, Vermont, almost completed a sewing machine which he invented in 1818. His conscience would not let him continue, however, when he realized that his invention would put many hard-working tailors out of business.

The first continuous-stitch sewing machine was patented in 1851 by Isaac M. Singer, founder of the Singer Manufacturing Company.

First Home Lit by Electricity

Although several other claims have been made for this record, it appears to us that the first person to equip his home with electric lights was Moses G. Farmer of Boscawen, New Hampshire, who turned on the power in 1858. Farmer is also credited with the invention of the fire-alarm telegraph system.

First Town Lit by Electricity

The first town to be commercially lit by high-tension electric current was Great Barrington, Massachusetts. The Westinghouse Company supplied the power in 1886.

Courtesy of MIT Historical Collections

First Electric Motor

Thomas Davenport, a blacksmith in Brandon, Vermont, pieced together the first electric motor in 1834. He used whatever materials were at hand, and took a thread to wind the armature.

Largest Telephones

Hall's Jumbo Telephones, measuring ten inches in diameter, are the largest phones ever made. They were issued by an electric supply house in Boston, Massachusetts, around 1895 as a device to transmit voices short distances. Based on the tin can and string principle, these membrane telephones or "lovers" were able to operate up to 170 yards.

First Rocking Skate

James Plimpton, Westfield, Massachusetts, machinist and acclaimed "Father of Roller Skating," revolutionized the roller skate by developing one that could turn (or rock). Prior to Plimpton's introduction of the rocking skate, roller skates were used primarily by children inside the home. Plimpton's skates became popular for women, enabling them to take genteel exercise out-of-doors. His design became an immediate success when patented in 1863.

First Snowmobile

Virgil D. White of West Ossipee, New Hampshire, invented the first snowmobile in 1913. A garage and automobile mechanic, White saw a future for a snow vehicle that could pilot children to school in the winter, carry mail, and transport doctors to snowbound rural areas. He built the snowmobile from the chassis of an old Ford and adapted tractor-like treads to the rear and two runners to the front. His Snowmobile Company, Inc.* turned out about 3,500 per year. White, as vice president and general manager of the company, ran the factory, which was located in West Ossipee. (The snowmobile boasts yet another first! It was the first practical ski tow, used to drag skiers to the top of a mountain.)

**Another market opened for the Snowmobile Company, Inc. The people in the Great Sahara Desert wanted something to replace the temperamental camel as a means of cross-desert transportation. The little factory in West Ossipee made sandmobiles, the first in the world, and shipped them to Africa.*

First Steam Bicycle

Sylvester H. Roper of Francestown, New Hampshire, invented a number of things in his day, but his best remembered creation was America's first practical steam bicycle. A well-known experimenter of steam propulsion in the late nineteenth century, Roper entered his steam-powered bicycle in a race at Boston's Charles River track on June 2, 1896, when he was seventy-three years old. People laughed at the old man's fire-eating, smoke-belching machine, but as the pressure in the bicycle's boiler rose to 180 pounds (the same amount used later on to power locomotives!), Roper left the other racers behind and the spectators changed their tune. The bicycle circled the track in two minutes, one and two-fifth seconds, a phenomenal time. Urged to beat his own record, Roper set off for one more try. He reached forty miles per hour, but then veered off the track and landed in a ditch. He had died suddenly of a heart attack.

First "Real" Automobile

On April 19, 1892, Charles Duryea tested America's first gasoline buggy on the streets of Springfield, Massachusetts. On June 11, 1895, he received a patent for the "World's First Real Automobile." It was the first motorized vehicle to use an electric ignition and a spray carburetor. Charles Duryea accomplished all this before he had reached the age of thirty! He went on to improve his early car and in September, 1895, he established America's first motorcar corporation, the Duryea Motor Wagon Company. His office was located on Taylor Street, and when he opened for business, Duryea also became the first person in New England to sell cars on a regular basis.

First Gasoline-Powered Vehicle

The first gasoline-powered vehicle in New England made its first appearance on the streets of Providence, Rhode Island. It was a streetcar built by G.B. Brayton in 1873.

First Tractor Tread

In 1900, a tractor named "Mary Ann," and a special tread to fit her, were invented by Alvin Orland Lombard of Waterville, Maine. The steam-powered machine, originally used to haul logs, was the first lag tractor; when equipped with treads, it took a place in history as the forerunner of the bulldozer.

First Mountain-Climbing Railroad

In 1869, a cog railroad train reached the summit of Mt. Washington (New Hampshire) and became the first train in the world to successfully climb a mountain. It all started back in 1852, when Sylvester Marsh, a native of Campton, New Hampshire, climbed the mountain on foot. He enjoyed the view, but thought the hike was a little too strenuous. So, he decided to run a railroad up the mountain.

He built a model and with enthusiasm developed the rack rail and cog wheel engine, using $139,000 of his own capital. Neither ridicule nor the Civil War could lessen his ambitions. The first locomotive for the railroad was made in Boston and shipped to Littleton, New Hampshire, and from there hauled in pieces by teams of oxen twenty-five miles to the base of the mountain. When assembled, it was nicknamed "Peppersass" for its resemblance to an old-fashioned peppersauce bottle (see photo above). The bottle-like portion or boiler was mounted on trunnions to keep it vertical, regardless of grade. It had no tender, so wood for fuel was picked up along the way.

The first passenger trip to the summit occurred on July 4, 1869. During its early years in service, Peppersass was accompanied by three other vertical boiler locomotives, with an enclosed cab and much larger cog wheel in the rear. In 1878, much-improved horizontal boiler engines were adopted.

After Marsh's death, the railroad changed hands and equipment several times. It still runs, and thus holds another record as the oldest mountain-climbing railroad in the world.

Largest Locomotive

Steamtown U S A in Bellows Falls, Vermont, has an extensive collection of old trains which includes "Big Boy," the largest locomotive on earth. In 1941, twenty five of these giants were built for Union Pacific to haul freight and troops over the Rocky Mountains. Big Boy weighs a staggering 1,200,000 pounds, and has to be moved frequently so it doesn't sink into the ground.

Most Unsuccessful Train Engine

Locomotive No. 1 of the Boynton Bicycle Company, built in 1889, was the most unsuccessful railroad engine ever constructed in New England. Although E. Moody Boynton's basic ideas were sound — his conception of a lightweight train which would be able to travel at 100 miles per hour and required a telephone system was a prelude to more modern designs — his little engine never worked. It was light enough, and its almost total lack of friction did enable it to move at high speeds, but it had no power, and was incapable of pulling any cars.

Worst Train Wreck

The worst train wreck ever to occur in New England was the four-train pileup in the train yard of East Thompson, Connecticut, on December 4, 1891. As the Southbridge Branch local stood on the westbound main track of the busy yard, eastbound train No. 10 plowed into it. Then eastbound train No. 8 crashed into the back of the pileup. By this point it was too late to try to warn the boat train, which ran into the accumulating wreckage in the darkness. The most amazing thing about the wreck, however, is that, despite the tremendous damage, only two people were killed.

Only Rabbit Train

So-called because of the common opinion that it was possible to go rabbit hunting during her delays and still be back in plenty of time to continue the journey, Train No. 582 was New England's only "Rabbit Train." She ran between Springfield and Athol, Massachusetts, from August 1, 1880, to June 1, 1935.

Smallest Railroad

Rides on the smallest train in the world were taken seriously by vacationing passengers in Old Orchard, Maine. In the summer of 1899, everyone succumbed to the charm of the six-foot miniature steam locomotive that was built on the deck of the resort's Steel Pier. For five cents, anyone could ride from the main entrance of the pier straight out over the ocean for a full third of a mile.

First Stanley Steamer

Francis Edgar Stanley of Newton, Massachusetts, built the first Stanley Steamer, which bears his name. (His wife injured herself while riding a bicycle and the accident inspired the buggy as a safer way to travel.) In 1897, he drove the completed car down Washington Street in Newton. Later, Stanley and his wife made history as the first motorists to drive to the top of Mount Washington — a feat indeed, considering there were no paved roads at the time. By 1917, the Stanley Steamer had grown to a five-passenger, twenty-horsepower touring car listed for $2,200.

First Flying Machine

On June 12, 1878, the first powered, lighter-than-air machine was taken up over Hartford, Connecticut. The operator, Mr. Quindlen, weighed only ninety-six pounds and sat suspended from a steel rod underneath the twenty-five foot gas cylinder. With double handles he turned a cog-edged steel wheel that powered a four-bladed horizontal fan directly beneath him. The fan caused the machine to ascend and descend. On the first trip Quindlen demonstrated the vehicle's power to change altitude and direction. He managed to return the ship to its starting place, to the amazement of everyone present. The following day, Quindlen made a nine-mile trip from Hartford to Newington; taking about fifty minutes, he estimated that the air ship's highest altitude was 2,000 feet.

First Airplane Flight

Numerous Connecticut historical associations and the 9315th Air Force Reserve Squadron have uncovered documents, drawings, photographs, and various paraphernalia which prove to them that Gustave Alvin Whitehead was the first to fly an aircraft. The Fairfield resident flew (as recorded in the *Bridgeport Sunday Herald* of August 18, 1901) his No. 21 airplane at Tunxis Hill in Fairfield on the fourteenth of August two years prior to the Wright brothers' flight. Whitehead is denounced by the Smithsonian Institute because there are no photographs of him in flight. Even if his claim isn't accepted by the authorities, he had numerous aeronautical firsts to his credit: he was the first to use landing wheels on his aircraft; the first to use aluminum in his engines and propellers; the first to experiment with pitched propellers and air-cooled engines; and the first in America to use concrete runways!

Last "Gee Bee"

The last surviving example in the United States of the Granville Brothers Model A airplane, the "Gee Bee," is located at the Bradley Air Museum at the airport in Windsor Locks, Connecticut.

First Helicopter

Igor Sikorsky of Stratford, Connecticut, made great headway in the field of aircraft and flying when he invented the first helicopter in 1939. Eight years later, Sikorsky also designed the first four-engine amphibian airplane named "American Clipper."

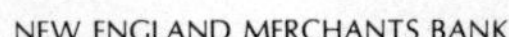
NEW ENGLAND MERCHANTS BANK

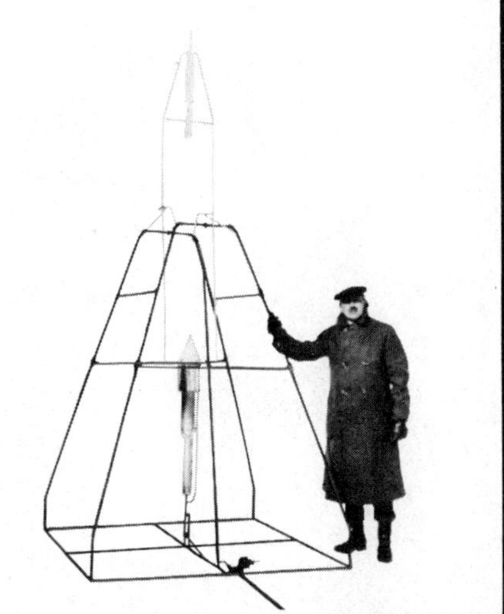

NEW ENGLAND MERCHANTS BANK

First Liquid Fuel Rocket

Robert H. Goddard launched the first liquid-propelled rocket on March 16, 1926. The rocket, fueled by liquid oxygen and gasoline, reached an altitude of forty-one feet and flew a length of 184 feet from its blast-off spot at a friend's farm in Auburn, Massachusetts.

First Air Retrieval System

Starting in 1953, and improving his design a number of times, Robert Edison Fulton, Jr. designed Skyhook, the country's first aerial retrieval system. His synchronized equipment, used by the US Air Force Aerospace Rescue and Recovery Service to pick up downed aircrews, can lift up to 5,000 pounds on one line. Fulton, from Newtown, Connecticut, is the great-great-great-grandson of the famous "Steamboat" Fulton.

Only Mower-Powered Hovercraft

When he was a sophomore in high school, Geary Siroonian of Weymouth, Massachusetts, "borrowed" the motor from his family's lawn mower and used it to power his homemade hovercraft, an air-cushioned vehicle that rides over land or water on a sixteen-inch cushion of air. The inverted saucer, ten feet in diameter, can cruise at speeds up to thirty miles per hour, and is the only vehicle of its kind we have heard of in New England.

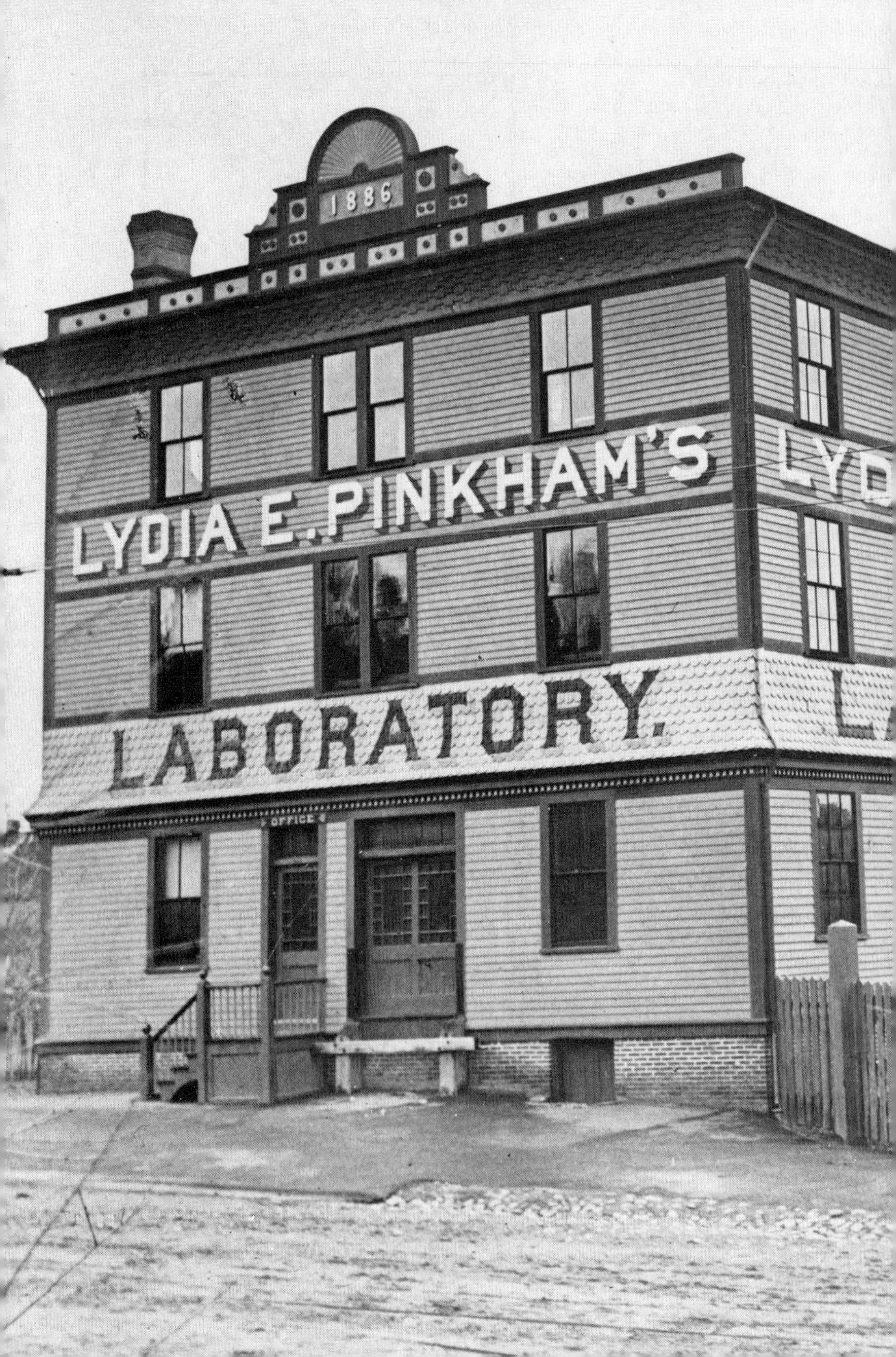
1886
LYDIA E. PINKHAM'S
LABORATORY.
OFFICE

3
Economic Endeavors

Oldest Business in Vermont

From its inception in 1813, the tradition of the E.T. & H.K. Ide Milling Company has been handed down from father to son, establishing it as the oldest continuously operated family business in Vermont. It began as a simple mill in Passumpsic, Vermont, where farmers would bring their corn or oats. The company still caters to local farmers.

Oldest Potato Chip Business

Starting as a caterer who provided meals for seashore travelers in Massachusetts, George Sleeper soon became known for the best part of his boxed lunches: his potato chips. Not the type to let an opportunity slip by, Sleeper began manufacturing potato chips by the barrelful, and selling them to local merchants. His successor, the John Boyd Potato Chip Company of Lynn, Massachusetts, continues the tradition as the oldest potato chip manufacturer in the country.

Largest Cooperage

Fremont, New Hampshire, is the home of Spaulding and Frost, the largest barrel manufacturer in New England. Operating since 1870, the business is the only New England barrel maker to use white pine exclusively. The company has also created the largest barrel in New England, which stands just under sixteen feet tall, holds slightly under 10,000 gallons, and weighs close to 2,000 pounds. On exhibit outside the factory, it is too large to fit through the door.

In the late 1800's, Lydia Pinkham's elixer, New England's most famous medicine, was manufactured in the building shown at left.

Oldest Nail Company

Established in 1819 by Issac and Jared Pratt on the site of an old cotton mill, the Parker Mills Nail Company furnished the country with nails formed from local iron ore. Although the company has undergone considerable changes since its founding in 1819 — it has moved several times and changed its name to the Tremont Nail Company — it still produces nails in Wareham, Massachusetts, making it the oldest nail company in the country.

Oldest Iron Works

Built in 1646, the Saugus Iron Works in Saugus, Massachusetts, was the first iron forge in the country. The works only operated until the late 1690s, but has been restored and is now open to the public as a National Historic Site.

Largest Monument Manufacturer

The Rock of Ages Craftsman Center in Barre, Vermont, is the largest and most modern self-contained monument manufacturing plant in the world, producing headstones, memorials and mausoleums.

Last Stoneware Pottery Maker

Dorchester Pottery is the country's last true stoneware producer, firing whole clay at a high temperature. The company opened in 1895 and still produces pots.

First Patent

In 1643, the first patent in the United States was issued by the Great and General Court of Boston to Joseph Jenkes of Lynn, Massachusetts, for an improved water wheel. It was described as "Engins of mils to go by water for speedy dispatch of much worke with few hands."

First Baby Carriage Company

The first New England company to manufacture baby carriages on a commercial basis was the F.A. Whitney Carriage Company, established in Leominster, Massachusetts, in 1858. One of the very early carriages, pictured here, was pushed along with the child facing back; later models had an open front so the passenger could see where he or she was going. Having developed the first reversible carriage handle in 1876,as well as the first long carriage handle, the company built the first vehicle for quadruplets for Mrs. Michael Salzo of New Haven, Connecticut, in May of 1921.

First Starch Mill

Erected in Wilton, New Hampshire, in 1811-12 by Deacon Ezra Abbot and his brother, Squire Samuel Abbot, the first starch mill in the country was run by water power. Starch, used in those days for everything from sizing cotton shirts to thickening pudding, was extracted from locally grown potatoes.

GREAT DEBATE

Oldest Snuff Mill?

Both the Byfield Snuff Mill in Byfield, Massachusetts, and the Gilbert Stuart Birthplace in Saunderstown, Rhode Island, claim to have not only the oldest but the *only* snuff mill in New England. Sensing a certain discrepancy, we examined each mill's claim to fame, and have finally resolved the controversy. The Gilbert Stuart Birthplace mill is the earlier of the two, having opened for business in 1750; but it was shut down for a considerable stretch of time before being restored and reopened in 1930. As a matter of fact, so much time had elapsed since the original operating days of the mill that completely new equipment had to be installed before production could resume.

The Byfield Snuff Mill, although not operational until 1804, hasn't ever ceased production and so rates as New England's oldest snuff mill in continuous operation.

Oldest Unaltered Brick Mill

The Belknap Mill in Laconia, New Hampshire, was built in 1823, and is the oldest brick textile mill in the country.

First Chocolate Mill

Located beside the Neponset River in the Lower Mills section of Dorchester, Massachusetts, America's first chocolate mill began operation in 1765. The mill, once famous as the headquarters of the Walter Baker Company, is no longer in operation.

First Sawmill

New England's first sawmill was built in 1823, in Fitzwilliam, New Hampshire. A project masterminded by Hezekiah Stone as a service to his neighbors, the sawmill was built at a point where the Priest River narrowed. By damming the river, Stone created a pond and built the mill on it.

Smallest Paper Mill

Operating for approximately two years in the early 1960s, the smallest paper mill in New England was located in the basement of a house in Great Barrington, Massachusetts. Royal Moore, a craftsman whose hobby is studying the art of making paper, was commissioned by Sheldon Fink, an artist who had just moved to Alford, Massachusetts, to fabricate quality paper for a book of etchings that Fink wanted to publish. Moore no longer makes paper on a regular basis. "It is," as he says, "just a hobby."

Last of the Great Mills

Once the largest mill in the world and once the world's largest producer of cotton goods, Amoskeag Industries is the last of the huge New England mills still standing. Organized in 1810, the company made Manchester, New Hampshire, one of the first American cities to be built up around an industry.

Providing space for homes, tenements, and a commercial district, the Amoskeag Manufacturing Company planned the placement of streets, public commons, a cemetery, municipal buildings, and churches as the city expanded. The first mill buildings went up in 1838, the last one in 1915, but the continuity in style won the mill company fame throughout the world. Serious competition from southern cotton manufacturers and the onslaught of the Great Depression forced the once-thriving mill to close in 1935.

Oldest Machine Shop

As far as we can tell, the Moffett Mill on Great Road in Lincoln, Rhode Island, is the oldest machine shop in New England. Records say it was built around 1812.

First Spinning Machine

Samuel Slater built America's first successful spinning machines in Pawtucket, Rhode Island, in 1790. Having apprenticed in a textile mill in Derbyshire, England, Slater had no blueprints to work from but he did have an accurate memory and an inventive genius. Funded by the public-spirited Moses Brown of Providence, Slater built his cotton mill on the banks of the Blackstone River and surprised even the English, who had guarded their invention so carefully.

First Cotton Gin

Eli Whitney revolutionized American agriculture and manufacturing with his production of the first cotton gins in New Haven, Connecticut, in 1794. Whitney's company, however, was out of business by 1797, since many southern planters refused to pay the required percentage of their cotton yield, preferring instead to copy the simple design of the mill.

First Hooked Rug Patterns

In 1868, working from his red peddler's wagon in Biddeford, Maine, Ed Frost sold the first commercial hooked rug patterns. Women were just beginning to accept bright hooked rugs when Frost came out with commercial patterns that became so popular he gave up his wagon and moved to Boston to expand the business. Most of the hooked rugs hanging in museums and collections today were made from a Frost pattern.

Oldest Pattern Company

Ebenezer Butterick, working in the mid 1800s as a tailor in Sterling, Massachusetts, developed the idea of using paper patterns to make clothing. Sold nationwide to tailors and dressmakers, the first patterns were hand cut in Butterick's home and packaged in boxes of 100. After patenting his idea in 1863, Butterick moved his business to New York City, where it is known as the Butterick Fashion Marketing Company.

First Straw Bonnet Maker

Betsey Baker of Providence, Rhode Island, produced the country's first straw bonnet in 1798, when she was only twelve years old. Known from that point on as a braider, she nevertheless refused to take out a patent on the process; as a good Christian, she was determined that her name should never go to Congress!

First Buttons

In 1719, Phineas Bradley of New Haven, Connecticut, became the first person to manufacture buttons in New England.

First Pewter Buttons

The country's first pewter buttons were manufactured by O. & O. Robinson in Attleboro, Massachusetts, in 1812.

First Brass Button

In 1802, Abel Porter & Company was the first concern in the country to produce brass buttons. Working with the Grilley brothers in Waterbury, Connecticut, the group formed the basis of what is now the Scovill Manufacturing Company.

First Drugstore

Although no longer in its New England location, Caswell, Massey & Co. was America's first drugstore, established in Newport, Rhode Island, in 1752. It was here that George Washington ordered two bottles of Number Six cologne to be shipped to General Lafayette in France.

First Combs

Captain Robert Cook, a resident of Needham, Massachusetts, made the first horn combs about which there is written record sometime previous to 1756. The founding of the comb industry in New England, and America, is credited to Enoch Noyes of West Newbury, Massachusetts, who made his first combs in 1759 and then taught his skill to many other workmen. By 1775, the comb industry had moved to Leominster, Massachusetts, and that city went on to become the largest comb manufacturer in the country.

First Toothbrushes

After moving to Haydenville, Massachusetts, in 1843, Alfred Critchlow laid the foundations of the Pro-phy-lac-tic Brush Company, the country's first independent toothbrush company. Now located in Florence, Massachusetts, the business goes by the name of the Pro Brush Division of Vistron Corporation, owned by the Standard Oil Company.

Oldest Grocery Store

A country store founded in Chepachet, Rhode Island, in 1809, has long been considered to be America's oldest continuously operating grocery store (or store that sells groceries), despite claims from several other parts of New England. After investigating the evidence on all sides of the issue, we agree that the store, now known as Brown and Hopkins, does indeed deserve to hold the record. Its historic storefront, little changed today, is shown above as it looked in 1867, when it went by the name of Horace Kimball General Store.

Last Upcountry Yankee Peddler

Although there were an estimated 16,594 tin peddlers in the United States in 1860, by the early 1900s H.B. Swett of Pittsfield, New Hampshire, was the last true Yankee peddler. He traveled in Maine, Vermont, and New Hampshire.

Last Pounded Ash Basket Maker

Benjamin Higgins of Chesterfield, New Hampshire, the last Yankee craftsman to form sturdy baskets with a painstaking age-old technique, retired unofficially in 1966, after more than sixty years of continuous work. His pounded ash baskets were meticulously constructed from separated strips of ash cut from whole trees.

First Yankee Peddlers

Edward and William Pattison of Berlin, Connecticut, became the first true Yankee peddlers. In the 1740s they made the country's first tinware, and vended their trinkets to colonial housewives.

Shrewdest Peddler

The shrewdest true Yankee peddler was John Boynton, born in Mason, New Hampshire, on May 31, 1791. Combining tinsmithing with door-to-door peddling of his own japanned tinware, he had made enough money by 1825 to set up a tin shop in Templeton, Massachusetts. Eventually he became sales manager of a whole fleet of red peddler's carts, and after twenty years of diligent industry, he retired as a very wealthy man, devoting his considerable funds and energies to philanthropic ends, including the founding of Worcester Polytechnic Institute.

Last Old-Fashioned Egg Man

In his horse-drawn cart, Bert Southwick delivers eggs and vegetables to the people of Northfield, New Hampshire, and is the last old-fashioned egg man in New England. Southwick continues to use his pinto mare and enclosed milk wagon for practical, rather than purely nostalgic, reasons; he can make the 100-or-so stops each day in about half the time that it would take him in a truck.

First Mail-Order Man

As a ploy to keep her young son from enlisting in the Civil War, in 1866 Mrs. Thompson of Bridgewater, Connecticut, suggested he run a small advertisement in the local paper offering a free prize to those who would sell packets of notepaper for him. The idea skyrocketed and Charles Benjamin Thompson became the first mail-order businessman. From notepaper he branched out to mail-order soap, and so overwhelming was the demand for this product that he was forced to open his own factory. By 1900, the business was thriving and the federal government changed Bridgewater's post office rating from fourth class to first class. It was reported that one day more mail was shipped out of Bridgewater than out of New York City.

First Offshore Lobsterman

William Whipple, ordained as a Methodist minister after graduating from the Boston University School of Theology in 1958, went on to become the country's first commercial offshore lobster fisherman. Founding the Prelude Corporation of Westport, Massachusetts, Whipple was the first to take so many lobsters from waters 130 miles offshore.

Most Famous Medicine

Although in the mid 1800s anyone with a black satchel and some herbs could call himself a doctor, the remedial qualities of Lydia E. Pinkham's Vegetable Compound, produced in Lynn, Massachusetts, made it the most famous medicine ever to come out of New England. And the easily identifiable picture of Mrs. Pinkham on the label, used from 1876 on, can be cited as the most famous trademark of its kind. The miracle tonic for "all those painful complaints and weaknesses" was produced until 1974.

First Witch Hazel

A man from Connecticut is credited with purchasing the recipe for witch hazel from an Indian. The balm was much in demand and the fellow made quite a bundle for himself manufacturing and selling the formula.

First Seed Packets

The first people to market herb seeds in small paper packets were the Shakers, whose seeds came on the market sometime in the early 1800s.

Largest Artificial Flower Company

California Artificial Flower Company, located in Cranston, Rhode Island, is the world's largest manufacturer of artificial flowers.

Oldest Garden Center

Berkshire Garden Center in Stockbridge, Massachusetts, was founded in 1931, making it the oldest such establishment in New England.

CANNING RECORDS

First to Can Vegetables

After convincing his slightly reticent brother-in-law, Caleb Jones, to plant a small field of sweet corn near Portland, Maine, Isaac Winslow became the first person in the country to can vegetables. The year was 1839.

First Patents

Thomas Kensett, Sr. and his brother-in-law, Ezra Daggett, of New Haven and Cheshire, Connecticut, were the first to receive a patent on a hermetically sealed can in the early 1800s. And in 1839, the same year that Isaac Winslow set his record, William Underwood patented the first true tin-plated canister.

First Food Technology

William Underwood and Samuel Prescott, having teamed up in 1895, were the first to develop a comprehensive theory on the sterilization of food, laying the groundwork for all further research on canning, freezing, and dehydration.

First and Oldest Cannery

When William Underwood opened the country's first cannery on Boston's Russia Wharf in 1920, he was the first to apply the new science of bacteriology to actual food processing. It was supposedly in Underwood's factory that the term "can" first came into common usage, when a rather lazy clerk grew tired of writing the entire term "canister" on each container of food. Now in Westwood, Massachusetts, the company is America's oldest continuously operating cannery.

Only Dandelion Canner

The W.S. Wells and Son Canning Company in Wilton, Maine, is the only company in the country that cans dandelion greens. Packing fiddleheads and dandelions since 1896, the company continues its down East philosophy that if the fish are biting, the harvesting can always wait a day or two. (Women at work in the cannery are shown at right.)

Oldest Food Trademark

William Underwood Company's trademark, the ubiquitous red devil, is the oldest registered food trademark still in use in the United States today. First used in 1867, it was assigned No. 82 by the US Patent Office in 1870, and has been updated six times since.

First Frozen Food

Clarence Birdseye of Gloucester, Massachusetts, introduced the world's first frozen food in 1925. His innovative research affected the habits and lifestyle of the entire nation.

Oldest Candy Company

When Mrs. Spencer arrived in Salem, Massachusetts, from England in 1806, without a penny to her name, her neighbors supplied her with a barrel of sugar, and the enterprising lady founded New England's first candy company. Mrs. Spencer immediately whipped up a batch of "Gibralters" to sell outside the old First Church and did so well that she was soon in business for herself. Located at 122 Derby Street in Salem, Massachusetts, Ye Olde Pepper Companie still has a jar of Mrs. Spencer's original Gilbralters, 145 years old and still tasty! (These candies must also be the oldest to be preserved in New England.)

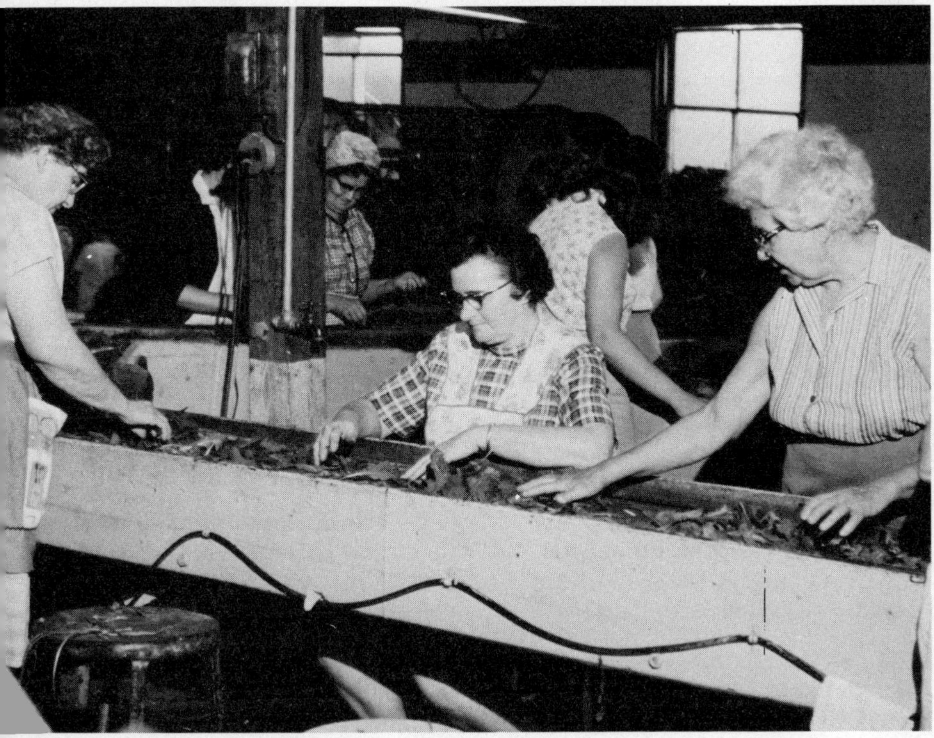

Largest Cymbal Producer

The Zildjian family of Norwell, Massachusetts, produces approximately ninety percent of the cymbals being used in the world today. Originating in 1623 in Turkey when an alchemist named Avedis discovered a secret combination of metal alloys that would deliver a clear sound when formed into cymbals, the business — and the secret of the formula — has been handed down to each succeeding generation of the family. In 1928, Avedis Zildjian of Quincy inherited the business and began to manufacture the instruments in Massachusetts. It appears that the secret of the mixture is still safe: a team of scientists from MIT tried to chemically analyze and reconstruct a Zildjian cymbal, but could not.

Courtesy of Paul J. Reale

R.J. SPILLANE

Oldest Toy Drum Manufacturer

Founded in 1854 by a mechanic/inventor and a promoter/salesman, the Noble & Cooley Company of Granville, Massachusetts, is New England's oldest toy drum company in continuous operation. Silas Noble and James P. Cooley started the business in Noble's farmhouse kitchen but were so immediately prosperous that they built their first factory less than two years later. Since the Civil War, the factory has concentrated on toy drums.

Last Wooden Hobbyhorse Maker

The Whitney Reed Chair Company of Leominster, Massachusetts, was the last self-contained business in New England (and we think in all of the country) to produce wooden hobbyhorses. The company's last president, Herb Green, retired in the 1950s, after trying without success to develop a plastic horse with the charm and appeal of the wooden ones.

First Playing Card Manufacturer

Jazania Ford (or Foord), living on Highland Street in Milton, Massachusetts, in the late 1700s and early 1800s, was the first person in America to produce playing cards. The first cards issued were "commemorative cards," with scenes depicting great moments on the backs.

First Catnip Mouse

Although no longer in existence, Ludlam's Pet Shop of 69 Bromfield Street in Boston, Massachusetts, was the birthplace of the catnip mouse. Evelyn Ludlam Conroy, whose father owned and operated the shop, decided that her cats would probably prefer something softer than the catnip-filled wooden balls her father sold. The idea was so popular that she was able to start her own business, the Waltham Catnip Mouse Company, in Belmont, Massachusetts.

First Geographical Globes

James Wilson manufactured America's first geographical globes in Bradford, Vermont, in 1812. After reading through eighteen volumes of the *Encyclopaedia Britannica,* the self-educated man produced his globe, which served as the prototype for a manufacturing company.

Only Wooden Christmas Cards

Yankee Artists of Keene, New Hampshire, is, to the best of our knowledge, the first and only manufacturer of wooden Christmas cards in New England. The idea, developed by Chris and Peter Booras in the late 1950s, involves using thin white wood from South America decorated by famous artists.

First Christmas Card Business

The first company to manufacture Christmas cards in America was founded by Louis Prang in 1875. Starting as the operator of an inauspicious lithography shop in Roxbury, Massachusetts, Prang later became known as the "Father of the American Christmas Card." The company's first cards were copied from popular British cards of the period, but grew more and more ornate over the years; many Prang cards are famous for their excellent reproductions of oil paintings.

First Valentines

Having received a token for St. Valentine's Day from a friend in England in 1847, Esther Howland of Worcester, Massachusetts, decided to fashion her own holiday cards. New England's first valentines, made from English or French note paper, or fashioned from household scraps of lace, paper, and ribbons, were put together in Howland's workshop by neighborhood girls. Several of the old valentines are retained in a collection at the American Antiquarian Society.

First Boston Directory

Complete with illuminating tidbits about residents and their occupations, the first Boston Directory was produced in Revolutionary War days as a guide to trade and commerce within the city. Fifty-three pages long, it included such names as Sam Adams, John Hancock, Paul Revere, and Charles Bulfinch.

First Cylindrical Letter Press

In 1790, using plans patented by William Nicholson of London, England, a Dr. Kinsley of Connecticut built New England's first cylindrical letter press.

First Union-Owned Company

Much to the astonishment of the international business community in 1959, the employees and the employees' union of the Merrimac Hat Company of Amesbury, Massachusetts, bought up the majority of shares of what was then the largest domestic producer of women's fur felt hat bodies. Their action made the business New England's first union-owned company. Merrimac Hat has since gone out of business.

GREAT DEBATE

First Printing Type Maker?

The first manufacturer of printing type, Mr. Mitchelson from Scotland, reportedly started his business in Boston, Massachusetts, in 1768. But some sources consider him to have been rather unprosperous. Accordingly, the honor of opening the country's first successful type foundry goes to Abel Muell (or Buell) of Killingworth, Connecticut, who established his shop in 1769. (Mr. Muell, a convicted counterfeiter, also minted the first official United States coin and engraved New England's first American map.) Even so, reports say that the process of forming type was not perfected until 1852, when Edwin Allen of South Wyndham, Connecticut, produced his machine for manufacturing wood type.

Most Professional Counterfeiters

Perhaps the neatest job of coin counterfeiting in all of New England was performed between 1829 and 1831 by a former government engraver named Ball and a Canadian printer and pressman named Thompson. Doing their work in two abandoned caves in the Maine wilderness, they milled pseudo-silver coins that were actually less than fifteen percent substandard. When their half-witted fence was trailed by the sheriff and a posse, Ball and Thompson quickly dumped most of their equipment into the lake and attempted a getaway. Seen before he could make the run, Ball shot the sheriff and was subsequently arrested and hanged. Thompson, and the rest of the coins and equipment, were never seen or heard from again.

First Mass Production

The first successful attempt at a mass production of interchangeable parts was Eli Whitney's production of 10,000 muskets for the federal government in 1801. Whitney was a native of New Haven, Connecticut, and had promised to deliver his muskets directly to the White House. Unfortunately, the guns were eight years late in delivery.

First Nuclear Power Plant

Rowe, Massachusetts, is the home of New England's first nuclear power plant. It was established in 1954 when ten regional investor-owned utilities announced the formation of Yankee Atomic Electric Company.

Strongest Glass

Although only in business from 1866 to 1890, the Lyndeboro Glass Company of South Lyndeboro, New Hampshire, manufactured material of such high quality that it was known as the strongest glass in the country.

First Pressed Glassware

The first pressed glassware in the country was manufactured by the Boston and Sandwich Glass Company in Sandwich, Massachusetts, about 1835. A museum in the town on Cape Cod exhibits pieces of the company's earliest work.

Worldliest Ice Trade

One of the better-known institutions in London, England, during the mid 1800s was the marketing of chunks of ice from Wenham Lake in Massachusetts. Since most ice in Britain at that time was formed on the sides of roads or in shallow, murky reservoirs, the pure ice from Wenham Lake was one of the foremost social necessities. The fact that the huge blocks managed to survive the month-long sea voyage from Massachusetts to London without melting was the source of innumerable discourses which ended only with a slight change in company management. Having discovered that it was cheaper to ship ice directly from Norway, company agents obtained the rights to ice from a lake near Oslo which they named Lake Wenham.

Largest Man-Made Water Supply

Quabbin Reservoir in central Massachusetts is the largest man-made domestic water supply impoundment in the world.

Last Ice House

Monte's Ice House in North Easton, Massachusetts, the last natural ice house in New England, closed in the mid 1960s. The company, run by Fred J. Monte, served dairies and small companies.

Last Buggy Whip Manufacturer

Founded in 1798 by Isaac Turner in Southfield, Massachusetts, Turner & Cook is the last company in the western hemisphere to manufacture buggy whips. The company owes its survival over the centuries to Julius Turner, who developed the first braiding machine (speeding up production and freeing many women from the cottage industry of braiding), and was the first to use rawhide instead of the customary scarce whale bone for the core of the whips.

GREAT DEBATE

America's First Canal?

Mother Brook, as the well-known waterway in Dedham, Massachusetts, is called, has long been acknowledged as the first man-made canal in America. This claim has been challenged in recent years by residents of Boston's South Shore who assert that the Cut River, running from Duxbury Bay north to Green Harbor, was actually the first man-made canal in the country. The Cut River, designed by the Pilgrims as a small boat's alternative to treacherous ocean travel, was begun in 1633; we can find no record, however, of the date that the canal was actually completed. While Mother Brook was not started until 1640, the fact that a mill was being built on the canal in 1641 indicates that the canal's construction proceeded fairly rapidly; it may conceivably have been operational before the Cut River. So the question of which canal was open first remains unresolved.

First Traction Canal

The Middlesex Canal, designed to transport cargo from Lowell, Massachusetts, to Boston, became the country's first traction canal when it was built and first used in 1803.

First Ford Dealer

Mr. Philip A. Williams, Jr., of Longmeadow, Massachusetts, established the first Ford dealership in New England on January 19, 1904. His salesroom was located at 147 Columbus Avenue in a then fashionable part of Boston.

Maine's Only Sulky Maker

The Maine Horse Supply Company of Greene, Maine, is the only manufacturer of racing sulkies and exercise carts in the state. Founded by Merle and Phyllis Hodgkins, Jr. in 1960, the company was a New England exclusive until a similar manufacturer set up shop in Connecticut.

First Bicycle Manufacturer

The Columbia Manufacturing Company turned out the country's first factory-made bicycle in Hartford, Connecticut, in 1877. The company then went on to become the country's first mass producer of mopeds.

Finest Steam-Driven Fire Engine

Boston purchased the country's first fire engine in 1678, a hand-operated device that was filled with water by a bucket brigade. This historic fact is certainly worth noting, but we'd also like to give mention to Engine No. 38, a steam-driven beauty that we think is the finest engine of its kind ever to be used in New England. It is shown here at a four-alarm blaze in front of the Boston Molasses Company on Summer Street in South Boston in 1911.

First Automobile Producers

In 1896, with a business called "Steam Wagon Makers," Fred Grout of Orange, Massachusetts, became the first man to manufacture automobiles in New England. His vehicle's boiler, capable of generating 225 pounds of pressure, was strategically located under the seat. Grout delivered one car per day in the height of production, to the tune of $2,500 to $4,000. He should have known a good thing when he had one; soon after switching from steam vehicles to gasoline-powered cars in 1907, Fred Grout was out of business.

Oldest Water Company

On February 22, 1798, nineteen residents of Durham, Connecticut, decided to buy the nearby Cold Spring and establish a water system to supply their homes. Still working by gravity to provide water to twelve homes on Main Street and one on Maiden Lane, the Durham Aqueduct Company is the oldest operating water company in New England.

First Public Transportation

A mile-long horsecar route in New Bedford, Massachusetts, that ran from the old railroad depot to the steamboat wharf in the early 1870s, was New England's first public transportation. The cars were used to help passengers arriving by steamboat from Nantucket and Martha's Vineyard transport their luggage to the railroad station. Since the horsecars were fairly slow and could not travel very far, they were soon replaced by the newer electric trolleys.

First Subway

Opened for service in the autumn of 1897, the transit system of Boston, Massachusetts, was the country's first underground transit line. The two-and-two-thirds mile tunnel came to be known as "The Elevated."

Last Five-Cent Ride

Biddeford and Saco Bus Lines, offering bus service between the two Maine towns, operated the last five-cent bus ride anywhere in America. In 1956, the line raised its fare to ten cents.

NANTUCKET

4
Ships and the Sea

First Mermaid
The first mermaid ever reported in New England was sighted by Captain John Smith off Monhegan Island in 1614.

First Commercial Ship
Launched in October of 1607 near the mouth of the Kennebec River in Popham, Maine, the *Virginia* was the first vessel constructed within the United States to be used solely for commercial purposes. She was also the first ship built in America by the English.

First China Trade Ship
Sailing into the harbor of Salem, Massachusetts, in May of 1787, the *Grand Turk* was the first New England ship to return from Canton, China, in the opening years of the American China trade. Carrying such goods as silk clothing and porcelain, the vessel set the stage for fifty years of American maritime prosperity.

First Submarine
America's first submarine was built by David Bushnell of Saybrook, Connecticut, in 1775. The *Turtle* was six feet high, constructed of oak timbers in the shape of a round keg, and held together with iron bands. In Washington's army, the submarine's first military task was to attach an explosive device to the hull of the British ship *Eagle*. Although the discovered presence of such an underwater craft seemed to alarm the British, the explosive device floated away from the hull of the ship before detonating.

The Nantucket, *resting in calm seas at left, is New England's last lightship. She is stationed where no mechanical buoy can replace her.*

First Circumnavigating Ship
Funded by several Boston merchants seeking to increase the American China trade, the 212-ton *Columbia* became the first American ship to sail completely around the world. Built at the Briggs Shipyard in Scituate, Massachusetts, she made the 41,900-mile trip in a mere forty months. Sailed by Captain Robert Gray of Tiverton, Rhode Island, she also set a record as the first ship to carry the American flag around the world.

First Canvas Canoe
Manufactured in Eastport, Maine, in the early 1800s, the first canvas canoe was put together by Clarence Sargent and a friend, both in their teens.

Oldest Commercial Sailing Vessel
Built in 1871, the *Stephen Taber,* a sixty-eight-foot, two-masted, gaff-rigged, coastal schooner, is the oldest documented commercial sailing vessel in the United States. Presently offering one-week cruises out of Camden, Maine, the ship originally transported lumber and brick along the New England coast.

Oldest Ferry
After examining several conflicting claims, it appears to us that the oldest ferry in continuous operation in the United States is the Rocky Hill line, which crosses the Connecticut River near Glastonbury, Connecticut. Having made its first run in 1655, the ferry was taken over by the Connecticut Department of Highways in 1915, and consists of a barge, fifty-eight feet long and fifteen feet wide, with a capacity for three cars, propelled by a thirty-foot towboat.

First Ocean-Going Iron Tug

In 1840, the first ocean-going, twin screw, iron tug boat was built by R.B. Forbes in Boston, Massachusetts.

First Steel Ship

The *Dirigo,* the first steel sailing vessel constructed in the United States, was launched at Bath, Maine, in 1894.

Largest Ship Model

The Whaling Museum in New Bedford, Massachusetts, houses the world's largest ship model, the eighty-nine-foot *Lagoda,* as well as the world's largest collection of whaling gear.

Most Wooden Ships

Maine has produced more wooden ships than any other state in New England.

Last Shipyard of Large Ships

Currently housing displays of machinery, tools, and small boats, the Percy and Small Shipyard of Bath, Maine, is the only surviving shipyard in the United States where large wooden sailing vessels were once built. It is now part of the Bath Marine Museum, and the tools and equipment originally used are on display.

Oldest Government Shipyard

Originally purchased on June 12, 1800, the Portsmouth Naval Shipyard is the oldest government-owned shipyard in the country. Although geographically located in Kittery, Maine, the shipyard's mail volume is too heavy for the small community, so its post office address is Portsmouth, New Hampshire.

PAUL A. DARLING

Last Great Wooden Ship Builder

Harvey Gamage of South Bristol, Maine, started his business in 1924, and was the last of the truly great builders of wooden ships. He began a gradual process of retirement in 1975, and constructed his last of 264 boats, a thirty-two-foot Friendship sloop named the *Lady,* completely on his own in a small shed on the grounds of his shipyard. A legend in his time, Harvey Gamage died in 1976.

GREAT DEBATE

Birthplace of the American Navy?

Marblehead, Massachusetts, so claim its loyal residents, is the birthplace of the American Navy, since the *Hannah,* the first ship to be commissioned into service by George Washington in September of 1775, was built in Marblehead and manned by a captain and crew from Marblehead. But the loyal residents of nearby Beverly contend that at the time of its first service, the fortuitous ship was moored within their town limits, a detail not overlooked by General Washington, who ordered the ship put to sea from Beverly.

The situation is further complicated by other towns' claims to the same honor, from Machias, Maine (whose ship, the *Unity,* had captured a British naval sloop in June of 1775), to Philadelphia, Pennsylvania, (where the Congress voted the birthplace of the Continental Navy in October of 1775).

Even the Navy, which has corroborated the claims of both Marblehead and Beverly at different points in history, seems unable to decide. In their most recent stand, a confirmation of a Beverly Historical Commission report in 1969, the Navy acknowledges Philadelphia as the birthplace of the Continental Navy and Beverly as the birthplace of General Washington's Navy. But the Marbleheaders are not yet convinced . . .

First True Ocean Yacht

Cleopatra's Barge, built in 1816, was the first American ocean-going yacht, possibly the most luxurious ever made, and an anomaly in her grim puritanical hometown of Salem, Massachusetts. The extravagance and exuberance with which the ship was fitted out and used reflected the character of her captain, George Crowninshield, Jr.

Although she traveled well under sail, she was decorated more in the fashion of an ornate mansion, with very unnautical names for each compartment such as the hall, the drawing room, and the master bedroom (complete with a fourposter bed). After the untimely death of George Crowninshield, the ship began a series of rather uneventful voyages, culminating her life with a flair worthy of old George, as the royal vessel for King Liholiho of Hawaii. Although *Cleopatra's Barge* met her fair end in the South Seas, the cabin saloon of the ship was returned to New England and is on permanent display at the Peabody Museum in Salem, Massachusetts.

First Extreme Clipper Ship

Built in 1851 to provide the fastest cargo transport possible between Boston and California, Boston's first extreme clipper was the *Flying Cloud.*

GREAT DEBATE

Fastest Clipper Ship?

Two remarkable ships stand out in New England history as the fastest clippers to have ever sailed the seas. The *Northern Light,* designed by Samuel Pook and launched from East Boston, Massachusetts, in 1851, made the trip from San Francisco to Boston in a record seventy-six days and six hours. The *Red Jacket,* launched in 1853 from Rockland, Maine, made the trip from New York City to Liverpool, England, in an amazing thirteen days, one hour, and twenty-five minutes. As the distances and times are impossible to compare, and neither ship is available for a sail-off, the title of the fastest clipper ship remains undecided.

Fastest Down-easter

Not quite as fast as the clipper ships from the same era, the fastest four-masted down-easter was the *Shenandoah,* built in Bath, Maine.

Last Wooden Whaling Ship

The *Charles W. Morgan,* built in 1841 and currently on display at Mystic Seaport in Mystic, Connecticut, is the last wooden whaling ship remaining in the United States. Designated a National Historic Landmark, she is 113 feet long, fully rigged, and in her prime could carry 13,000 square feet of sail. (Curiously enough, the *Morgan* was featured in a 1922 movie, "Down to the Sea in Ships," but her role was played by the *Wanderer.)*

Last Working Whaling Ship

A 116-foot, two-masted schooner, *The Wanderer,* was the last square-rigged whaling ship in the country. She was wrecked in June, 1924, after leaving New Bedford, Massachusetts, when she was driven up onto the nearby rocks of Cuttyhunk Island during a storm.

Nantucket Firsts

Captain Timothy Folger, a Nantucket mariner, was the first to chart the Gulf Stream. He passed his drawing along to his cousin, Benjamin Franklin, who had it engraved on a copper plate.

Nantucket was the first deep-sea whaling port in colonial America.

The Siasconset Wireless Station was the first to receive a wireless message to save lives at sea off the American coast; this incident involved the *Florida-Republic* collision in 1909.

The first surfboat built for lifesaving service in the United States was put together in Nantucket in 1806 by Captain Gideon Gardner for the Massachusetts Humane Society.

The first whaleship to be deliberately rammed and sunk by a whale was the *Essex* of Nantucket. Melville used this incident, which occurred in 1820, in his climax of *Moby Dick.*

The first American whaleship to enter the Pacific Ocean was the *Beaver* of Nantucket, which did so in 1701.

Unique to New England, the Nantucket beach vole (related to the field mouse), is found only on Muskeget Island. It is threatened not by humanity, but by the cats belonging to the lighthouse keeper.

Most Successful Fishing Schooner

Built in 1926 as the last of the Gloucester fishing schooners, the *Adventure* landed more fish than any schooner in the history of dory fishing. By 1953, when she retired from fishing to offer one-week cruises from Camden, Maine, she had already netted more than $3.5 million worth of seafood.

Largest Three-Masted Schooner

The largest three-masted schooner ever built was the *Bradford C. French,* launched off the New England coast in the late 1800s.

Largest Five-Masted Schooner

Launched in Bath, Maine, in July of 1903, the *Elizabeth Palmer* was the largest five-masted schooner ever built. She was not, however, the most durable; she was on the bottom of the sea by 1919.

Largest Six-Masted Schooner

The *Wyoming,* launched by Percy and Small Shipyard in Bath, Maine, in 1909, was the largest six-masted schooner ever built. She was over 329 feet long, over fifty feet wide, weighed 3,730 tons, and was the largest wooden sailing vessel to carry cargo in a United States fleet.

Only Seven-Masted Schooner

Constructed in Quincy, Massachusetts, in 1902, the *Thomas W. Lawson* was the only seven-masted schooner ever built. Weighing over 5,000 tons, she was sailed by a scant crew of sixteen men until lost in the Atlantic on December 13, 1907.

Most Durable Schooner

The *Cora F. Cressy*, built in Bath, Maine, in 1902, stayed afloat longer than any other big schooner — a full thirty years. One possible reason was her unusually high bow which reared forty feet out of the water even when fully loaded.

First Steamboat

In 1787, Captain Samuel Morey voyaged down the Connecticut River from Hartford, Connecticut, and on through the Long Island Sound to New York in "a little boat just large enough to contain himself, rude machinery connected with a steam boiler and a handful of wood for the fire." This was the first steamboat, a full thirteen years before Fulton's epic journey.

First Successful Steamboat

Affectionately dubbed "The Old Sawmill" by noise-conscious passengers, the *Vermont* was New England's first successful steamboat, built by John and James Winans, who also helped Fulton with his folly. The *Vermont* took to the waters of Lake Champlain in 1809 with much clanking and sputtering, advertising twenty-four-hour cruises of the lake which more commonly took the better part of a week.

Famed for her cantankerous, willful, and unpredictable nature, one of her original problems was the lack of adequate dock space at the various ports along the lake; passengers were forced to literally chase the ship in rowboats in order to clamber aboard. If they weren't run down they were safe, and thankful. If they were, the mishap would most probably be blamed on the cargo: the original steamboat could execute turns willingly enough, but heavy barrels, allowed to roll from side to side along the deck, helped tremendously. The pilot, when turning, would shout for deck clearance; the passengers would thereupon scramble for safety, deck hands would roll out the barrels within an instant.

Her most famous, most willful act, however, was also her last. After six years of exciting service she blew a hole in her hull when her engine exploded, and she promptly sank.

Courtesy of Barnett Fowler

Last Woodburning Steamboat

First launched in 1908 from Boothbay, Maine, the *Sabino* is the last steamboat in New England to burn wood and coal. Once making regular trips along the length of the east coast, the boat is now on display at a museum in Maine.

S.R. GILCREAST, JR.

Last Paddle Wheel Steamboat

Taken out of service in 1954, the *S.S. Ticonderoga* was the last paddle wheel steamboat in the United States. Having served as a passenger ship on Lake Champlain, she was hauled overland to her resting place at the Shelburne Museum in Shelburne, Vermont.

Only Ship to Return Century Later

The *Emma C. Berry,* launched in Noank, Connecticut, in 1866, sailed back to her original shipyard on July 4, 1966, becoming the only merchant ship to return to the site of her original launching an entire century later.

Oldest Lighthouse

Boston Light, the monument guarding the entrance to Boston harbor, is the oldest lighthouse in America, first lighted in 1713, and officially established as a government light on September 14, 1716.

Last Horseboat

The last horseboat in New England was operated by Horace Smith in the early 1800s. Used only on Lake Winnipesaukee in New Hampshire as a method of crossing the lake in any weather, the horseboat utilized two horses walking on a treadmill in the stern of the boat to turn the paddle wheels alongside. The treadmill itself was situated on a steep slant; the horses had to walk forward to keep from falling into the water.

Only Duck Boat

Constructed in an adult woodworking class by Lillian Schell of Braintree, Massachusetts, New England's only duck boat, fashioned to resemble a mallard, was completed in 1972. Mrs. Schell, a housewife and grandmother, is the only woman we know of in the region to have built a pedal-powered boat.

Only Swan Boats

Long famous as one of the first signs of spring in New England, the swan boats in Boston's Public Garden are the only boats of their kind in New England. Pedaled slowly and gracefully around the island in the center of the pond, the six boats have been managed by the Paget family since their origin in 1877.

Most Captains in One Family

A love for the sea must have penetrated the air in Brooksville, Maine, where the Tapley brothers were born. Of eight brothers who all went to sea following the Civil War, seven became sea captains. Once, four brothers, each in his own ship, were anchored simultaneously in China! Shown in photo are the amazing mariners. Front, left to right, Capt. Jerome Tapley and Capt. George Tapley. Rear, Capt. William Tapley, Capt. Robert Tapley, Deacon Tapley (the only brother who was not a captain), Capt. Abraham Tapley, Capt. Thomas Tapley, and Capt. John Tapley. The family surely holds a record for having the most captains!

Oldest Society of Sea Captains

Established in 1742, the Boston Marine Society in Boston, Massachusetts, is the oldest marine society in the country, and still meets regularly as a club.

Greatest Rescue Feat

The greatest single rescue feat in New England maritime history, to our way of thinking, was the daring effort of George Bloomer and his lifesaving crew to help a stranded schooner, the *Grecian*. The ship was wrecked off the shores of Chatham, Massachusetts, in 1885, in a severe squall, but "Crazy George" managed to run a lifeboat out through the waves to bring in the captain and several sailors.

Worst Winter Storms

As far as we can tell, the worst winter storms ever to hit the New England coast occurred between December 15, 1815, and January 31, 1816. During that period every issue of the newspapers listed one or more ships as wrecked or missing.

Largest Whirlpool

Churning into life whenever the wind and tides are right, Old Sow, in Passamaquoddy Bay near Quoddy, Maine, is undisputably the world's largest whirlpool. Created by the meeting of two tides and a dangerous back-eddy, the whirlpool has been known to swallow up entire four-masted schooners.

Most Controversial Cup Defender

When W. Starling Burgess was chosen by Harold Vanderbilt to build a ship to defend the America's Cup in 1930, he proceeded to design the most revolutionary racing sailboat ever to compete in the international series of races. Working at the Herreshoff plant in Bristol, Rhode Island, Burgess produced the *Enterprise,* which included a system of winches, an extremely wide boom, and a lightweight mast. Although the ship won the trials and the race easily, such mechanical devices threatened the very sporting nature of the race; underdeck winches and lightweight masts were subsequently barred from America's Cup competition.

First Transatlantic Rower

In May of 1876, Alfred "Johnny" Johnson, a halibut fisherman from Gloucester, Massachusetts, became the first man to sail a rowboat across the Atlantic Ocean. The journey from Gloucester to Liverpool, England, took him three months.

First Transatlantic Captain

Born in New London, Connecticut, in 1779, Moses Rogers became the first captain to maneuver a steamship across the Atlantic. His boat, the *Savannah,* made the epic journey in 1819.

Most Mysterious Wreck

On June 29, 1941, the *Don,* a forty-four-foot motor cruiser, left Bailey Island, Maine, with thirty-five passengers aboard, bound for a picnic on Monhegan Island. The ship never reached Monhegan; only thirteen bodies were recovered and no wreckage was ever found, making the *Don* the most mysterious wreck in New England history. Explanations of the disaster run from tales of a tremendous explosion to accounts of the ship sinking on a submerged ledge.

Safest Steamboat Line

The Fall River Line, unlike competing companies, was renowned for its record of passenger safety. In its entire history, the company lost only one passenger. G.H. Marsten died of a skull fracture following the collision of two Fall River Line steamers, the *Plymouth* and the *City of Taunton.*

Most Famous Ship Collision

The most famous ocean collision in New England was the sinking of the *Andrea Doria.* The New York-bound Italian luxury liner collided with a Swedish ship and sank off the coast of Nantucket on the night of July 25, 1956. Miraculously, only forty-five of the passengers died.

Worst Double Ship Disaster

Two huge tankers sank off Cape Cod, Massachusetts, on February 18-19, 1952; it was the worst double disaster in New England maritime history. As Coast Guard rescue planes were responding to a distress call from the *Fort Mercer,* a pilot discovered the *Pendleton,* also sinking fast, which had been unable to radio.

Most Avoidable Steamship Disaster

When the steamship *Portland* set out on November 26, 1898, for her regular journey from Boston, Massachusetts, to Portland, Maine, her pilot, Captain Blanchard, knew that they would be faced with one of the worst November blizzards of all time. Renowned for his ability and his cautious weather outlooks, he advised his employer to cancel the voyage, but had been reprimanded by his steamship company and ordered to set sail in spite of the storm, to get the passengers home after their Thanksgiving weekend. The ship, however, never made it to Portland; she sank in the storm and all 200 people on board perished.

Last Lightship

While there were well over a dozen lightships flanking the New England coast at the turn of the century, the only one which has not been replaced by some sort of a mechanized buoy is the *Nantucket.* Located beside the busiest shipping lane in the world (off the Nantucket coast), the ship cannot be replaced by a buoy because she sits too far out at sea, the ocean bottom is too soft, and the water is much too deep. The present *Nantucket* is the twelfth ship to be stationed there since 1854, all the others falling victim to ice storms, high seas, dense fog, and heavy traffic.

5
Memorable Moments

Most Holidays

New England, unlike other regions in the United States, celebrates nineteen holidays throughout the year, seven of which are strictly Yankee affairs. While not all are observed by each state, it would be possible to enjoy an average of one official holiday every three weeks by tripping around the six states. The unique events include: *Patriots Day* in Maine and Massachusetts, April 19; *Bunker Hill Day* in Boston and Suffolk County, June 17; *Evacuation Day* in Boston and Suffolk County, March 17; *Fast Day,* the oldest of strictly Yankee holidays, observed only in New Hampshire, the fourth Monday in April; *Vermont's Town Meeting Day,* first Tuesday in March; *Bennington Battle Day* in Vermont, August 16; and *Rhode Island's Declaration of Independence Day,* May 4.

First Christmas Celebration

Sixteen years prior to the landing of the Pilgrims, the first Christmas was celebrated in New England. It was a far cry from what we associate Christmas to be today but nevertheless, it was merry. Frenchmen Champlain, DeMonts, and their venturous men enjoyed roast venison and stewed rabbit on a small island at the mouth of the St. Croix River, about sixteen miles south of Calais, Maine. The account of this story is noted in *Champlain's Journal.* Worship in the newly finished chapel and holiday merry-making in characteristic French fashion were the special features of that day.

At left, one of the region's fastest frogs at the annual Mark Twain Jumping Frog Contest, New England's only such competition.

First Singing of America

The Park Street Church in Boston claims to be the first place where the patriotic song "America" was sung. Supposedly on July 4, 1832, several hundred children assembled at the church to attend a patriotic celebration. The new song, written only five months prior, was featured on the program, but did not become widely popular until the time of the Civil War when it inspired enlistments.

Biggest Bomb to Bomb

Nearly 400,000 Americans congregated in Boston for the fireworks display on the nation's 201st birthday, July 4, 1977. This particular display had advertised the firing of the largest fireworks shell ever to be exploded on the East Coast. It was scheduled to go off from the Charles River at approximately 10:40 PM. The shell, weighing 126 pounds and capable of achieving a height of ten times that of any standard shell, never went off. The rocket, apparently a dud, bombed out, much to the disappointment of the large, patriotic crowd.

Boston's First Fourth

Boston's first Fourth of July celebration did not happen on July 4, 1776, but rather, on July 18, 1776. News didn't travel very fast in the eighteenth century and the adopting of the *Declaration of Independence* on July 4, 1776, did not trickle north until several weeks later. An actual copy of the *Declaration* arrived early in the morning on July 18 and citizens flocked to the Old State House to hear Tom Crafts, the Suffolk County Sheriff, read it. By evening, all insignia of the crown had been torn down and added to the large bonfire on King Street.

Grandest Fourth of July Events

New England's grandest, most magnificent Fourth of July celebrations can be attributed to Henry C. Bowen of Woodstock, Connecticut. Nicknamed the "Prince of Patriots," Bowen personally directed and produced patriotic celebrations, the likes of which no one had ever seen before, for twenty-six consecutive years. A philanthropist, Bowen transformed a marsh in Woodstock to a recreation area known as Roseland Park. Here the festivities took place. Outdoor band concerts and games were held as well as a recitation of the *Declaration of Independence,* and poetry by John Greenleaf Whittier. Prominent people including four presidents spoke on contemporary issues. Strawberry shortcake and gallons of lemonade were consumed by hundreds of spectators who traveled from miles away to attend. The day's grand finale was a fireworks display — Bengal lights, asteroid rockets, twelve-foot Roman candles, and golden stars were just some of the lighted wonders shipped from Japan for the occasion. Bowen died in 1896 while preparing his next Fourth of July festival, and no continuous celebration of the same caliber has been staged since his death.

Oldest Fourth of July Parade

The nation's oldest continuous Fourth of July parade is held in Bristol, Rhode Island. Fourteen divisions, twenty-five floats, and thirty bands contribute to this Independence Day celebration.

First Macy's Parade

Although Macy's Department Store is associated with the New York area, its Fifth Avenue Thanksgiving Day parade is world famous for its extravagance and excitement. But the very first Macy's parade occurred in Haverhill, Massachusetts, the home of Rowland Hussey Macy before he moved to New York.

Macy's Wholesale and Retail Dry Goods House in Haverhill was struggling to survive, so Macy decided he must do something drastic to call attention to his business. In 1857, Macy planned a Fourth of July celebration. His idea was to have a simple band march from the downtown area up the street to his shop, and there a notable gentleman named Wilkins would deliver a patriotic address. More music would follow and the event would end.

The Fourth of July couldn't have been hotter so the band did not attract the crowds it had anticipated. The few onlookers followed the musicians down the street, but Wilkins had not arrived. In his absence, Macy decided to deliver the public address. He recited "George Washington, Soldier and Statesman," a speech he had memorized in his school days. The band played a few more selections and the concert ended. A year later, Macy and his wife moved to New York where he opened his successful department store and planned more parades.

Courtesy of Richard Pritchett

First National Thanksgiving

Sarah Joseph Hale was a hardworking woman with a great deal of determination for finishing projects started by other people. She was instrumental in establishing Bunker Hill Monument, in restoring Mount Vernon, and she is also credited as author of "Mary Had a Little Lamb." But she is best remembered today for what she did about Thanksgiving. Although celebrated as a tradition throughout the country, nobody could agree on one universal day for Thanksgiving. Every state opted for home rule, and established the holiday as each saw fit. Sarah Hale's campaign to establish a national holiday eventually reached President Lincoln, who, on October 3, 1863, issued an official proclamation:

"... I do, therefore, invite my fellow citizens in every part of the United States and also those that are at sea or who are sojourning in foreign lands to set apart and serve the last Thursday of November next, a day of Thanksgiving and praise to the Beneficent Father ..." Mrs. Hale had won and a national Thanksgiving had been proclaimed. Lincoln's successors maintained the tradition as long as Sarah Hale was living. It is interesting to speculate what Mrs. Hale might have said in 1939, the year President Franklin D. Roosevelt moved Thanksgiving to the third Thursday in November in order to add an extra week of shopping to the Christmas season!

C.S. GURNEY

Biggest Explosion

The blowing up of Henderson's Point in Portsmouth, New Hampshire, on July 22, 1905, was the greatest engineering feat as well as the biggest explosion ever seen up to that time. The point, a rocky protrusion stretching some 540 feet into the Piscataqua River until its fated day, was a treacherous obstruction to the ships headed for the US Navy Yard at Kittery, Maine. One dynamite blast was all that it took to blow the stone dam to fragments. Water flew up to seventy-five feet and the debris went as high as 170 feet. Fifty tons of explosives were used to lift the estimated 70,000 tons of rock. A ten-foot tidal wave was created from the returning water. Invitations were sent out by the company in charge of the blasting and 35,000 people came to witness the blow-up. Many others, less curious, fled on trains and trolleys out of Portsmouth, New Hampshire, for fear that either the whole city would be destroyed or a tidal wave would drown them all.

Largest American Flag

With a length of 366½ feet, a height of 193 feet, stripes measuring fifteen feet wide, and stars eleven feet in diameter, the largest flag in the world, one-and-a half times the size of a football field, was designed in New England as the brainchild of Len Silverfine of Warren, Vermont. Designed for the Bicentennial, the flag was made of nylon taffeta and when finished was 71,000 square feet and weighed one-and-a-half tons. Silverfine made elaborate plans for the hanging of the flag on the Verrazano-Narrows Bridge at the entrance of New York Harbor. It seemed only appropriate to hang the largest flag from the longest suspension bridge in the world. The flag was unfurled for a test raising on June 28, 1976, two days before the official hoisting. Eight mechanical winches pulled it more than 250 feet straight up, but engineers and soon everyone involved realized there was no way to get it down. The wind plastered the flag against the suspension cables, and as the gust's velocity increased, it exerted more and more pressure. The flag ripped, first one tear, then others, until the wind carried immense pieces away and desperate workmen pulled others in by hand. Although the flag never flew for the welcoming of the Tall Ships and the Bicentennial celebrations, it was the largest flag that was ever made.

Largest Light Festival

New England's largest light festival can be seen at Constitution Plaza in Hartford, Connecticut. Beginning the day after Thanksgiving, the light display continues through New Year's Day, kicking off the holiday season. The seventy-five-foot Christmas tree is decorated with 3,200 lights, each ten watts. Smaller lights of half a watt each, numbering 150,000, light up the smaller trees throughout the plaza. The fountain area is aglow with 6,000 bulbs, each with an intensity of three-and-a-half watts, all blinking in a sequence. The lights are turned on at dusk and shut off at ten o'clock for thirty-nine continuous nights. In recent years, Constitution Plaza has cut its festival by twenty-five percent in accordance with the energy shortage.

Only Ecumenical Blessing of Fleet

The Blessing of the Fleet ceremony in New Bedford, Massachusetts, an annual event, is the only one of its kind in New England to have clergymen of all denominations jointly presiding.

Loudest Sound of Music

From June 15 to 19, 1869, the Grand National Peace Jubilee held at St. James Square in Boston produced the loudest sound of music ever heard in North America. Performances in the Coliseum, the largest building erected up to that time, featured a chorus of 10,000 accompanied by an orchestra of 1,000, an organ thirty feet high, an anvil chorus sounding on 100 real anvils, and the largest drum ever seen in the world. Electrically fired artillery added to the program.

Patrick Sardfield Gilmore was the originator of this colossal concert. (Composer of "When Johnny Comes Marching Home," Gilmore took the pen name Louis Lambert.) Despite criticism and overshadowing pessimism, his Peace Jubilee was an outrageous success and Gilmore received world-wide fame. Throngs of people flooded the Coliseum and Boston had never seen such crowds. President Ulysses S. Grant made an appearance at the second day's performance.

Courtesy of Carol W. Kimball

First Country Fair

One day in 1807, an enterprising Yankee displayed his two Merino sheep in the elm-sheltered square of Pittsfield, Massachusetts, promoting New England's first country fair. Born in 1758, Elkanah Watson was no farmer by profession but his early business career was marked by a series of unusual "promotions." It wasn't until he failed at several projects in New York State that he moved his family to a farm in Pittsfield, Massachusetts. Buying two French Merino sheep from a US diplomat, Watson installed these as breeding stock on his farm, and later announced that the animals would be put on public display. The exhibit not only created comment but also started farmers in the Merino sheep business. Watson began to wonder what would happen if he showed larger domestic animals. Buying a prize English bull and short-legged pigs, he barnstormed the county, drumming up support for a professional cattle show. After three years, Watson had convinced twenty-six of the most progressive farmers to participate in the first agricultural exhibit — the Berkshire Cattle Show, later known as the Berkshire Fair and Cattle Show.

Smallest World's Fair

Every autumn, the smallest world's fair comes to Tunbridge, Vermont. One of the oldest country fairs, it received its sovereign right to operate directly from George III on February 3, 1761. Organized and owned by the Union Agricultural Society, it is an accepted part of every citizen's duty to work for the fair and make it a success. Exhibits range from the best kept livestock to prize winter wheat, homemade crafts, homemade syrup, jams and pastries.

Only Dowsing Convention

New England's only dowsing convention is held each year in Danville, Vermont, during the foliage season. Started in 1958, the American Society of Dowsers, sponsor of the event, takes itself quite seriously. Although their main goal is seeking water, today's dowsers believe anything from archaeological ruins to lost cats may be found with the divining rod.

Biggest Egg Festival

Each year, Maine throws the biggest egg festival in the United States. The Central Maine Egg Festival is held in honor of the State of Maine, the largest egg producing state in New England, which is ranked close to first in the country.

Only Jumping Frog Contest

The annual Mark Twain Jumping Frog Contest in Hartford, Connecticut, is the only contest of its kind in New England. In 1955, the first contest had two contenders; today more than 100 frogs compete. The winner, determined by yardage, gets a chance to sit on the throne of Dan'l Webster, hero of Mark Twain's story, *The Celebrated Jumping Frog of Calaveras County.*

Oldest Bathing Beauty Contest

Miss Winnipesaukee Bathing Beauty Contest, held annually in August, is the oldest contest of its kind in New England.

Largest Twin Party

One hundred sixty-seven pairs of twins registered at New England's largest twin party in Lakewood, Maine, held in the summer of 1938. The party featured records such as the prettiest, the most alike, the shortest, and the tallest. The event was planned by Welton P. Farrow for his twin brother, Harold, and several other twin-oriented people who formed a committee.

First Public Clambake

The first public clambake was held at Buttonwoods, Rhode Island, in 1839, as a publicity stunt during Benjamin Harrison's presidential campaign.

Largest Meal Eaten

The New England record for food consumption is held by two professional wrestlers, Andre and Tanakas, who stopped by Custy's Restaurant in North Kingstown, Rhode Island, a few years ago to take advantage of his "all you can eat" offer. Each consumed forty lobsters.

Largest Flock of Hawks

On September 20 or 21, 1756, what was perhaps the largest flock of hawks ever assembled flew across New England. It is recorded that twenty people saw this unusual occurrence, reported as follows: "... there was seen near Fort Dummer (Vermont) two large companies of pigeon hawks, judged to be about 4,000 in number, headed by two large eagles, one eagle heading one company and the other eagle the other. They found themselves too large for two companies and so divided themselves into four battalions. They fought over from Fort Hinsdell to Fort Dummer, and fighting from one fort to another for the space of four hours, till one company conquered the other, and chas'd after them." This is the earliest account of hawk migration printed in New World literature.

CHRIS MAYNARD

Largest Game Supper

In 1957, members of the United Church of Christ in Bradford, Vermont, decided to hold a game supper to raise money. Since that time, the event has become the largest game supper in the country. The first meal fed about 100 people; by 1977 the supper attracted more than 1,000. A staff of 100 workers dishes out some 2,000 pounds of meat and 800 pounds of vegetables each year. The menu includes venison, beaver, coon, wild boar, moose, pheasant, rabbit, bear, and occasionally antelope, elk, and duck, plus less exotic items such as squash, potatoes, and gingerbread.

RADIO FIRSTS

The world's first radio broadcast occurred on Christmas Eve, 1906. Sent by Reginald Aubrey Fessenden from a station in Marshfield, Massachusetts, the broadcast included the singing of "O Holy Night."

WGI-AM was the only radio station in New England prior to 1920. Located in Medford, Massachusetts, it held broadcasts for only a few hours a day, featuring classical piano music and any chitchat the announcer had to offer. There were no commercials since they hadn't been invented yet.

On September 21, 1921, WBZ in Boston, Massachusetts, became the first radio station in the country to be issued a commercial license to broadcast.

The first college lectures broadcast on radio originated from Tufts University and were produced by WGI.

"Short Story Writing" by Dr. J. Berg Esenwein, the country's first radio lecture series, was aired on WBZ Radio, September 27, 1923.

WGI was the first radio station to include a weather report in their broadcast.

The first public radio warning of a hurricane was broadcast in 1938.

In 1921, Boston Mayor James Michael Curley made the first political speech ever broadcast in the nation at the Medford, Massachusetts, station of WGI.

The first children's program was produced by WGI.

Broadcasting from the Home Beautiful Exposition in Boston, WBZ aired the first radio wedding on April 29, 1924.

The first automatic hourly "beep" to be broadcast by radio east of Chicago was produced in the fall of 1927 by WBZ.

First Weather Forecaster

E.B. Rideout, a native of Cambridge, Massachusetts, was the country's first official radio weather forecaster. Although his early employment was in the field of printing, Rideout spent all of his lunch hours at the US Weather Bureau office in Boston, learning all he could about meteorology. He worked as a weather observer for the bureau during World War I, but had to return to his printing job when the war ended and the regular observer reclaimed his position. Rideout was soon asked to join the newly formed American Meteorological Society, however, and after writing several letters to the Boston radio station WEEI about the connection between thunderstorms and static and radio waves, he was asked to make a few talks on weather over the air. This was the beginning of a long career of radio weather forecasting for him, for he stayed with WEEI, making regular weather broadcasts, for thirty-eight years. He is pictured here as he appeared during his 32,350th broadcast in his thirtieth year at WEEI in August, 1955.

Stock market reports were first broadcast by WGI as part of their news format.

The radio dramas that entertained the country before the advent of television were first started at the WGI station.

The first ice hockey game was broadcast on radio December 1, 1924.

The first baseball games to be heard over radio were the 1923 World Series. WBZ aired the series.

WGI was the first station in the country to air religious programs.

From the Marconi Station at the Cape Cod National Seashore in South Wellfleet, Massachusetts, the first two-way transatlantic radio transmission was made in 1903.

Radio's first official broadcast meteorologist cast his predictions from Boston, Massachusetts.

WBZ was the first radio station to sponsor the ground control approach system used in aircraft transport.

Calvin Coolidge was to the best of our knowledge the first United States president to make an official broadcast over the radio.

The first non-World Series baseball game to be heard over the radio was the New York Giants vs. the Boston Braves game, broadcast by WBZ radio from Braves Field in Boston.

The first Ford Hall Forum broadcast was aired by WBZ on October 19, 1924.

As early as 1921, WBZ became the first station to use any sort of remote pickup in radio broadcasting, and in 1928, the same station became the first in New England to use shortwave equipment for remote coverage. It has been operating ever since.

First Woman Broadcaster

Eunice Randall Thompson, shown above, was the first woman broadcaster to be heard over the air waves in New England. A native of Lovell, Maine, Thompson worked for WGI-AM in Medford, Massachusetts. Before this time, radio had been dominated by amateurs and small groups who delivered occasional broadcasts but made no consistent attempts at regular programing. This photograph of the proud Miss Thompson was taken at the radio station, around 1921.

Only Real Whale Ride

Although not many people are able to claim riding a finback whale, Frank Cabral, Jr., witnessed by his father, did just that and set a record in the process. Frank and his father, both lobstermen in Provincetown, Massachusetts, set out early one June morning in 1948 and started pulling up their pots, each in his own dory. Fishermen throughout the area reported seeing "Willie the Whale" but this was of no concern. On this particular morning, Willie made what was later interpreted as a friendly appearance, surfacing between the two boats.

Immediately afterward, Frank heard his father's call of warning, "Watch out for the whale — he's headed your way!" Within an instant, the sound of timbers cracking was all Frank heard, and suddenly he found himself ten feet in the air. Expecting to splash into the water, he was greatly surprised to find that he had landed on the back of the seventy-foot whale without a splash but rather a thud. He could feel the slick back of the beast under him as the whale moved forward and he slid backwards. Terrified and aghast, Frank finally fell into the ocean after what seemed like eternity. After fighting the undertow the huge creature left behind as he swam away, Frank managed to regain his strength and surface, only to see his partially submerged dory and the hole in it that the whale had made upon impact. So, young Cabral experienced the only real whale ride we've ever heard of.

Courtesy of Roger Hawthorne

First Car to Provincetown

In 1901, Charles Ayling drove a Stanley Steamer to Provincetown, Massachusetts, the first car to ever see that town. Taking eleven hours of on the road driving, Ayling and his Chestnut Hill neighbor, William Butler, made the record-breaking trip. At that time, the roads on Cape Cod were capable of handling only horses, so extra tires, tools, and lumber were brought along to enable the car to travel over the soft sand and deep holes. Upon reaching Provincetown, Ayling bought all the gas in town for the return trip. The two gallons cost seventy-five cents each.

First Car Across US

On a fifty-dollar wager, H. Nelson Jackson*, a Burlington, Vermont, physician, drove the first car across the United States. Starting in San Francisco on May 23, 1903, Jackson covered approximately 6,000 miles on his circuitous route through eleven states. Taking sixty-three days, he won the bet by twenty-eight days, but not without great expense. The car, a two-cylinder, twenty-horsepower, 1903 Winton with chain drive, right-hand steering, and a fragile-looking wooden body, caused a great amount of curiosity, enthusiasm, and mockery among all who happened to see it along its trip. Jackson, companion Sewall K. Crocker, and dog Bud arrived in New York on July 26, 1903, escorted by hordes of well wishers.

First All-Night TV Show

The first all-night TV program was aired by WCVB (Channel 5) in Needham, Massachusetts, on September 9, 1972. The show, hosted by George Fennell, is the only all-night program out of seven in the area that has a live host.

First Cable Landing

On July 23, 1869, the first French Atlantic Cable landed in Duxbury, Massachusetts. It stretched some 3,333 miles across the ocean from the far off station terminal in Brest, France.

Never before had a transatlantic cable run from Europe to the United States. The cable delivered five words per minute when first tested and the first words from America praised the Emperor Napoleon III on the successful termination of the enterprise; the return from France quoted a sharp rise in the price of cable shares on the Paris Bourse.

For many years the cable flourished at its maximum capacity of twenty words per minute. By 1930, however, it became outdated. The Cable Office at the corner of Washington and St. George streets was closed. Connected to the New York office of Western Union, the cable remains as a stand-by unit, ready if needed. But when the lease expires in 2006, the outdated cable will be left behind.

**Jackson is also Burlington, Vermont's, first traffic violator. He exceeded the city speed limit of six miles per hour and pleaded guilty to the charge.*

Worst Runaway Reservoir

On November 3, 1927, after long weeks of constant rain, the dam which confined the reservoir of Becket, Massachusetts, burst, and the resultant flood was the worst ever created by a released reservoir in New England history. The rain, surprisingly enough, had ceased that night, and when Fred Crochiere and Clint Ballou walked out to check on the dam at 3:30 AM, the water level had even subsided several inches. As they drew nearer to the structure, however, they saw a crevice two feet wide and almost twelve feet long forming along the top of the dam, and the sound of cracking and snapping became clearer. Barely escaping the explosion of the gatehouse, the men raced to the nearest house, and banged on the door until the residents woke up. After informing them of the danger, Ballou told the local operator to call everyone in low-lying areas of town, ordering them to evacuate momentarily. Ballou and Crochiere then continued their race through the center of town, alerting residents to the impending disaster. When the forty-foot wall of water broke through the dam and rushed over the town, it tore away all homes, factories, and railroad tracks in its path. With the exception of one woman who had outrightly refused to leave her house, no one in the town was killed, but most of the valley village was leveled.

Biggest Book Brigade

In order to solve a moving problem, the staff of the Windsor (Connecticut) Public Library organized what turned out to be the biggest book brigade in the country. By late morning, January 24, 1976, nearly 300 volunteers, including the governor, had rallied to the cause and managed to move 35,000 books in one day without boxes or moving vans. After breaking for lunch, the crew returned only to place the last book, H.G. Wells's *War of the Worlds* in its new quarters.

Loneliest Outpost

The observatory atop New Hampshire's Mount Washington provides the loneliest outpost in New England for the radio staffer who chooses to live there for part of the year, surrounded by extreme weather conditions. Hurricane winds (seventy-five miles per hour) occur more than 100 days per year. The lowest temperature ever recorded at the peak was forty-nine degrees below zero Fahrenheit. In 1934, wind velocity reached 231 miles per hour, a record for a surface station.

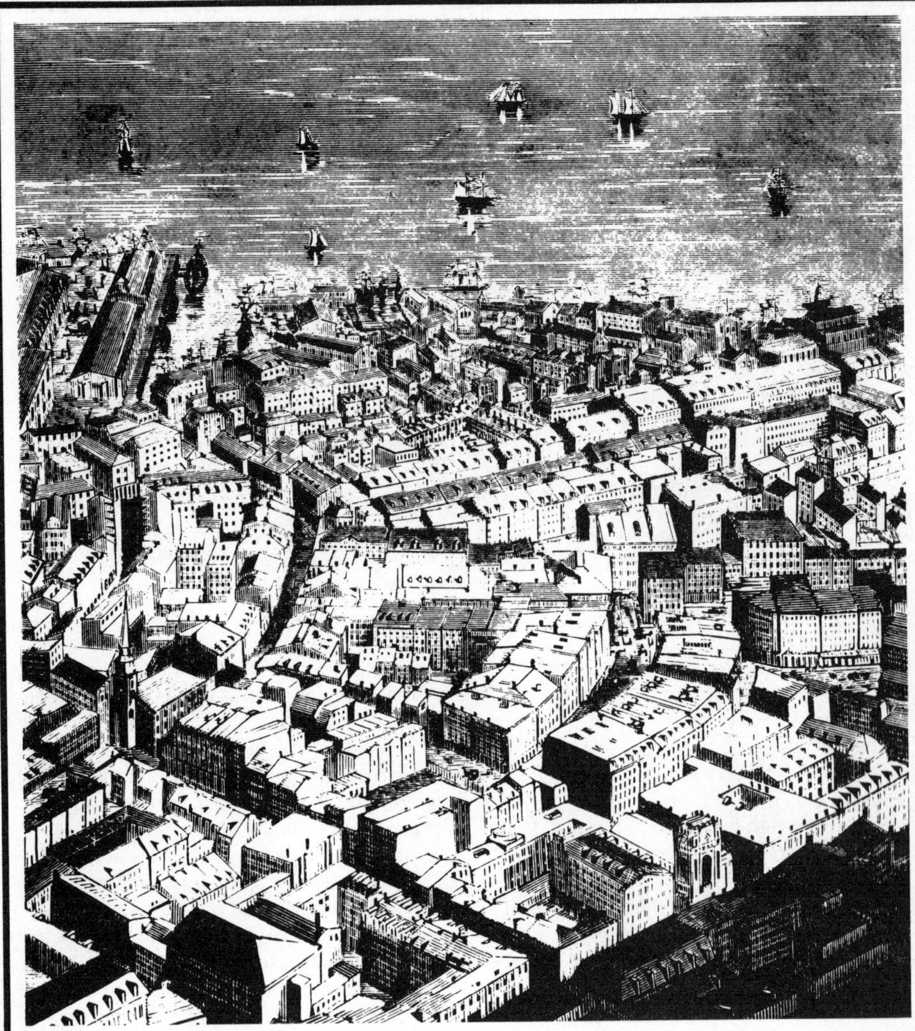

First Aerial Photograph

James Wallace Black, a Bostonian, is credited with taking America's first aerial photograph. On October 13, 1860, Black took the successful shot from a balloon over Boston Common. Mr. Black, a leading photographer of the day, had obtained plenty of experience taking pictures of prominent citizens and teaching the science of photography to many, including Oliver Wendell Holmes. After an initial attempt at photographing the Rhode Island State Capitol, Black made careful plans of all the minute details necessary for the flight in October. Suspended 1,200 feet in the air, he prepared and exposed eight negatives, one print coming out with extraordinary success. The procedure took about ninety minutes. Upon returning to Boston, Black printed several photographs from the only negative that had survived. He found that the outer limits of the picture included the Old South Meeting House on the left, Boston Harbor at the top, Summer Street at the right, and Winter Street at the bottom. (A sketch that was rendered from this famous original photo is shown here.)

First UFO Sighting

James Everell is recorded to have seen the first UFO in America on March 8, 1639, at Muddy River outside of Boston. He and two others, all claimed to be sober, discreet men, saw it flame up and become approximately three yards square. When it moved it took the shape of a pig and darted about for several hours.

First Hot Air Balloon School

As far as we know, New England's first hot air balloon school, known as Aerostats, was located outside of Hartford, Connecticut, and operated by Charlie MacArthur.

Largest Waterspout

Preceded by a smaller funnel of water which dropped from the clouds toward the sea, the largest waterspout ever recorded in New England history occurred on August 19, 1896, at 1 PM off Cottage City (now Oak Bluffs), on Martha's Vineyard, Massachusetts. Eyewitnesses reported that the diameter of the spout seemed to be 100 feet.

First Air Meet

The Harvard-Boston Aero Meet which took place in Atlantic, Massachusetts, in September, 1910, was the first air show of any significance. Among the contestants were Wilbur Wright, Glenn Curtiss, Walter Brookins, and seventeen-year-old Cromwell Dixon, who piloted his own small dirigible balloon. The superstar of the show and the favorite of the audience was the suave, articulate Englishman, Claude Grahame-White.

The events at the air meet included competition in speed, altitude, duration, spot landing, quick takeoff, and dropping imitation bombs. People of all ages came from miles around to watch. The *Boston Globe* donated $10,000 for the fastest time from the field to Boston Light and back, twice around; a total distance of thirty-three miles.

Grahame-White became the focal point of the show, winning all the contests and becoming the only contestant to fly to Boston Light. He was a hero in everyone's eyes and before returning to England, he accrued the fortune of $250,000 in prize money.

Strangest Hole in the Ice

You would be as startled as Bill McCarthy was had you looked out at a once frozen pond and found a three-foot gaping hole in the ice. In the winter of 1976-77, the ice on the McCarthy's pond had been frozen solid for over a month. Their horses had skipped fearlessly across it all day and suddenly it had been shattered as if with ease.

Such a bizarre occurrence created world-wide publicity for the McCarthy family and the small town of Wakefield, New Hampshire, where they lived. How this apparently perfect round hole got in the ice remains a mystery. The edges of the hole had melted from both the top and the bottom and the snow on the top of the pond had later turned to slush. None of the surrounding ice was broken and the pond's water was still.

Several explanations arose: some indicated that "top secret" testing had caused the hole; some romanticists decided to stick with the belief of UFOs; and others explained the incident through natural causes. A news release from the governor's office explained that the object "seen" by McCarthy was a shadow on the ice. Professor Alan L. Baker of the University of New Hampshire offered the explanation of meltholes in the ice.

WEATHER RECORDS

Worst Ice Storm

Thanksgiving weekend, November 26-29, 1921, witnessed the worst ice storm in New England. Hitting central and eastern Massachusetts the hardest, 3 inches of ice coated everything and immobilized the area for thirty-six hours. Power and telephone lines were down as well as trees. The forest loss in some areas was considered greater than that from the Hurricane of 1938.

Worst Hurricane on Cape Cod

September 14, 1944, $100 million worth of damage was created by the "Great Atlantic Hurricane" on Cape Cod. With winds higher than those reported in 1938, this storm hit only the Cape.

Worst Nontropical Storm

With hurricane intensity, the southeast gale of November 25-26, 1950, was the worst nontropical storm in New England. With gusts to 110 miles per hour and 160 mile-per-hour winds atop Mount Washington, the storm did considerable damage to the area.

Most Unique Storm

October 9, 1804, saw the most unique and damaging storm to ever hit New England. A medium-intensity, late-season hurricane was transformed into a heavy snowstorm. It destroyed the unharvested apple and potato crops, blew down large tracts of forest and toppled the spire of the Old North Church in Boston. A southward surge of cold air collided with an oncoming hurricane causing this unique and damaging storm.

Worst Tornado

The Sunapee Tornado of September 9, 1821, is recorded as New England's worst tornado in terms of intensity and length of its path. Forming on the west side of Sunapee, it crossed the lake and cut across the center of New Hampshire for twenty-five miles to Boscawen. It killed six people and was recorded to have blown away stones from walls that had been built with heavy boulders.

Worst Tornado in Terms of Loss

Worcester, Massachusetts, was the scene of New England's worst tornado in terms of casualties and property loss. Killing ninety people on June 9, 1953, it damaged $52 million worth of property.

Lowest Barometric Pressures of Nonhurricane Storm

On March 7, 1932, the barometer fell to 28.20 at Block Island and 28.45 at Boston in an otherwise undistinguished offshore gale that lacked the tightly wound center which would have yielded the very high winds associated with low pressures.

Worst Hailstorm

The worst hailstorm cut a path through three southeastern Connecticut towns on July 15, 1799.

Most Intensive Hailstorm

On August 23, 1916, in Sunapee Harbor, New Hampshire, hailstones averaging 1½ inches in diameter fell on an area of one to two miles for nearly thirty minutes. Raising foot-high waves on the lake as they splashed, the most intense hailstorm stripped trees of their foliage, destroyed gardens, and broke windows.

Highest Tide in Boston

The February, 1727, easterly gale created the highest tide in Boston. It pushed a sixteen-foot tide up the Charles River.

Worst Flood

The "Diane" floods triggered by rains from the dying hurricane caused the greatest property loss of any natural disaster. Over $800 million worth of loss was accrued in August, 1955.

Worst Flash Flood

On July 26, 1819, 15 to 20 inches of rain fell within a four to five-hour span causing the worst flash flood in New England. The flood affected a twenty-five square-mile area near Chester, Massachusetts.

Courtesy of Andrew E. Rothovius

Greatest Flood

Caused by two heavy warm rains, the March 9-18, 1936, flood totaled from 8 to 10 inches of rain within a ten-day period on a deep snow cover. The rains affected almost every stream in New England and raised the Connecticut River (37.6 feet at Hartford), the Merrimac, and the Kennebec to levels unapproached by any other flood.

Greatest Area Snowfall

The greatest snowfall over the widest extent of New England dumped 28.2 inches at the Blue Hill observatory and 56 inches in Long Falls Dam, Maine, on February 25-26, 1969. Hundreds of families were snowbound and road crews took as long as a week to clear the highways.

Worst Blizzard

New England's worst blizzard fell on March 12-14, 1888. New Haven, Connecticut, recorded 44.7 inches of snow; Middletown, Connecticut, claimed 50 inches, and Concord, New Hampshire, on the edge of the storm, had 27.5 inches.

Worst Blizzard in Maine

The worst blizzard in central and eastern Maine occurred December 30-31, 1962, with sub-zero winds and 46 inches of snow accumulating in Bangor.

Worst Blizzard in Berkshires

On March 2-3, 1947, 47-50 inches of snow fell on either side of the Massachusetts-Vermont border.

Worst Hurricane

The Hurricane of 1938 is the worst hurricane ever to hit New England. It made records throughout the country. The highest non-mountain wind velocity recorded was 121 miles per hour (sustained for five minutes), 160 mile-per-hour gusts were recorded at Blue Hill Observatory. When the death toll reached 586, it became the highest ever incurred by such an event in New England. The highest velocity of forward motion was recorded at 60 miles per hour and the highest storm surge was 20 feet in Providence, Rhode Island.

Only Molasses Flood

On January 15, 1919, the country's only molasses flood* occurred, creating damage so extensive it took six years to finally erase the vestiges of the tragedy. The scene was the low-lying section of Commercial Street between Copp's Hill and the playground in the North End of Boston. Near the sheds of the Boston and Worcester and Eastern Massachusetts railways, the paving division of the Public Works Department, the headquarters for Fire Boat 31, and the wharves with patrol boats and mine sweeps alongside, loomed the United States Alcohol Company's molasses tank, bulging with more than 2 million gallons of crude molasses.

Suddenly a low deep rumble shook the freight yard, the earth heaved and the sounds of ripping and tearing could be heard before a terrible boom was created as the bottom of the huge tank split open. The molasses was forced upward into a flume, creating an eight-foot tidal wave when it fell back to the ground. It crushed everything and everybody in its path. Filling the five-foot-deep loading pit, it began to creep over the warehouse door. Four loaded freight cars were whisked down the tracks and a half-filled car rode the crest of the wave like a child's toy boat. The molasses knocked down the iron corrugated walls of the freight terminal, and the doors and windows of the warehouse caved in with the pressure (two tons per square foot). The fire station was knocked over and pushed toward the ocean only to get caught on the pilings. Nearly twenty people lost their lives in the disaster and many more were injured.

**The hearings for the 125 lawsuits against the United States Alcohol Company set a record as being the longest in Massachusetts history.*

Boston's Worst Fire

On November 9, 1872, more than sixty-five acres and 547 buildings burned in the heart of Boston's business district. It was estimated that $75 million worth of property and merchandise was lost in the twenty-hour span that it took to control Boston's worst fire. Fire engines from twenty-one Massachusetts towns; Manchester and Portsmouth, New Hampshire; Newport, Rhode Island; and Norwich and New Haven, Connecticut, arrived in Boston to help.

Beset with problems from the start, the Boston Fire Department had been accused of having no training and inefficient facilities to cope with a fire of any size. Other circumstantial problems also arose. There was an epidemic of horse distemper and lung fever which limited the availability of horses to pull the fire engines. A massive crowd volunteered to hand-pull the engines through the streets of the city to catch the flames before they destroyed another building.

The fire reportedly started in the basement of the three-story Klous Building, numbers eighty-three, eighty-four and eighty-five Summer Street. A dry goods store, a necktie shop, and a manufacturer of bustles and hoopskirts housed in the building had quantities of combustible material. From the basement to the elevator and up each floor, the flames grew until they reached the roof. There, they leapt to neighboring buildings, melting lead and zinc in the mansard roofs and splintering the granite (supposedly fireproof).

New Hampshire's Worst Fire

The worst fire in New Hampshire's history occurred on May 4, 1930, in Nashua. Starting at the Boston and Maine Railroad bridge which crossed the Nashua River with a 200-foot span, it is thought to have been ignited either by a spark, a cigarette butt tossed from the window, or from kids playing craps near the bridge. Whatever the cause, an oil-soaked bridge instantly blew up in flames. In no time the fire reached either end of the bridge and proceeded to destroy a large section of the city. An entire area was left barren by nightfall except for the smouldering cellar holes and the water pipes spouting geysers. One report said that the fire swept a path three miles long and one mile wide. Some 1,500 people were left homeless and even more became jobless after the blaze demolished the business district.

Maine's Worst Fire

On August 15, 1907, the worst fire ever experienced in Maine consumed much of the seashore recreation area of Old Orchard Beach. Having broken out around 7 PM in one of the wooden hotels near the pier, the fire soon spread to many other hotels and destroyed much of the superstructure and booths and shops on the long pier.

Largest Fire Death Toll

On November 28, 1942, 492 people lost their lives in Boston's Coconut Grove fire. The death toll in this disaster was the largest of any fire in New England.

Most Firemen Killed

The Vendome Fire in Boston, Massachusetts, caused the greatest loss of firefighters in the twentieth century. A total of nine were killed on June 17, 1972, the same day the Watergate Building was broken into.

Boston's Worst Trolley Wreck

It was dusk on Tuesday, November 7, 1916, when car 393, the boxcar type trolley, plunged into Fort Point Channel, creating the worst streetcar accident in Boston's history. The car was full to capacity on its way to the station at Washington and Summer streets when the tragedy occurred. The drawbridge attendant had closed the gate barring the way to traffic, and had supposedly placed the red lantern on the barricade. Gerald Walsh, conductor, claimed no light was on. He failed to stop the streetcar at the open bridge, and it crashed into the channel. Car 393's brakes were of questionable reliability. The car slid forty feet but the brakes failed even after Walsh had tried to throw the car into reverse. Of the sixty-two passengers, only fifteen survived, including Walsh.

New Hampshire's Worst Trolley Wreck

Several events contributed to New Hampshire's worst trolley wreck: a sleepy attendant at Pelham Center; a thunderstorm the previous day that had upset the railway block signal system; and the motormen and the conductors relying on verbal signals were the causes for the collision of car 125 and car 137, on September 6, 1903. Car 125, with fifty-nine passengers, was moving as fast as possible to make up for a delay when it crashed into car 137 which was heading away from Pelham Center on an understood order. According to the conductor of the latter car, the carhouse operator, Oral Stevens, had given him the go-ahead. (Actually he had not.) After a futile attempt at chasing car 137 and cutting the circuit breaker to try to stop the electric flow, Stevens and all around heard the explosive crash. Six people were killed and many others were maimed and wounded. The blame for the tragedy was put on the starter, a motorman, and a conductor.

Most Daring Bank Robbery

Northampton, Massachusetts, will always remember what happened early on the morning of January 26, 1876. It was on that particular morning that more than a million dollars in cash and securities were stolen from the "burglarproof" vault of the Northampton National Bank. Not even the Brink's case equaled this crime in skillfulness and sheer melodrama.

The most daring part of this case was what happened at John Whittelsey's house the morning of the robbery. Whittelsey, cashier of the bank, was awakened at two in the morning by a person saying, "Be quiet and no harm will come to you." Seven men had invaded the home, gagging and binding the six other adults who lived there. Whittelsey was taken downstairs, held at gunpoint, and told to relinquish the combinations to the three locks on the vault. Trying to mislead his captors only proved painful for the cashier and he offered the information they desired. He was then blindfolded and gagged like the others.

Through the help of a greedy locksmith, William Edson, who had installed the bank's vault door, six men managed to get away with a vast amount of money without damaging the bank or injuring a soul. But a smart clerk at the bank who was deprived of a copy of the combination put the pieces together and implicated Edson as the chief accomplice. Edson turned state's evidence in order to escape a jail sentence, but several of his co-robbers were never caught. The bank received $700,000 from the estimated $1.25 million originally stolen.

Biggest Cash Robbery

A mail truck carrying $1,551,277 in cash from Cape Cod to the Federal Reserve in Boston was robbed of its contents on August 14, 1962, and the event became the biggest cash robbery in the country's banking history.

About fifty people from the banks and the postal service knew of this practice and were familiar with the routes the truck took, so the heist was easy to plan. The money was abducted in Plymouth by five bandits, one dressed in a state troopers uniform. Supposedly there were more people involved in the scheming but only five of the possible crooks were used for the actual holdup.

After five years, two men and a woman were finally indicted by the postal service. John (Red) Kelley of Watertown, who years later turned state's evidence on just about every crime except the Plymouth robbery, was acquitted, along with Mrs. Patricia Diaferio of West Roxbury, on insufficient evidence. Thomas Richards of Weymouth disappeared the weekend before his trial never to be seen again (he is presumed dead). Therefore, no one has been convicted and the case remains unsolved. Not one dime of the $1.5 million has ever been recovered.

Last Duel

Although carried out on a field in Marlborough, Maryland, the last legal duel fought in the United States involved a gentleman from Maine named Jonathan Cilley. The event brought to an end young Cilley's promising career as a representative for the newly formed State of Maine.

Only Funeral for a Horse

Although we have no date for this unusual event, it is said that the people of Rockport, Massachusetts, held a public funeral for a horse named Captain. The citizens of Cape Ann all knew Captain, who traveled with Dr. William Hackell on his daily routine. After long years of service, the horse died and the people of Rockport felt he deserved a proper burial. Placed in a large wooden box specially made for him, Captain was taken to the shore by sledge and dropped into the ocean with the outgoing tide, never to be seen again.

Longest Funeral

The longest funeral ever given to an American citizen was held for George Peabody of Danvers, Massachusetts. Peabody, a philanthropist, spent the last twenty years of his life giving away large sums of money, totaling $10 million.

He was pronounced dead on November 4, 1869, in London. Queen Victoria proclaimed November 12 as a national day of mourning and England put on a lavish funeral. Peabody's body was permitted to lie in state at Westminster Abbey, an unusual honor for an American. Then, on December 11, after cannon salutes, speeches, and honors, his body was placed aboard Britain's newest battleship, the *HMS Monarch,* whose exterior and interior had been painted black for the occasion. A special chapel was modeled from the cabin and the *Monarch* lay in Portsmouth Harbor until December 21, when more honors were paid.

Meanwhile the Americans, not aware of British plans, sent the *USS Plymouth* to retrieve the body. Upon arriving in England the *Plymouth* realized the British intentions and agreed to officially escort the *Monarch* on her way back to America.

On January 25, 1870, the two ships arrived in Portland, Maine, with more gun salutes. The public viewed the body for two days and it was transferred with lavish ceremony to the public auditorium for several more days of tribute. On February 1, George Peabody was transported by special funeral train to Peabody, Massachusetts, and the final funeral service was held at Harmony Grove Cemetery in Salem on February 8, 1870, three months later!

6
Famous Folk

First to Die in King Philip's War

Zechariah Smith was ambushed by a band of Indians in Dedham, Massachusetts, on April 12, 1671, and became the first man to die in King Philip's War. Smith was on his way to Providence when the incident occurred.

First to Die in Revolution

As far as we can tell, William French, a twenty-two-year-old patriot, was the first man shot to death in the American Revolution. On March 13, 1775, just before midnight, he fell, mortally wounded by five bullets, at the courthouse in Westminster, Vermont, following a skirmish with Tories.

First to Die at Bunker Hill

According to reliable sources, the first patriot soldier to fall at the Battle of Bunker Hill, June 17, 1775, was Asa Pollard of North Billerica, Massachusetts.

Oldest to Enlist in Revolution

Patriotic fever ran high in New England during the days of the Revolutionary War. Henry Francisco didn't let his accumulated years dampen his enthusiasm and he enlisted in the army in 1771, at the age of ninety-one, making history as the oldest man to enlist in that war . . . and, we bet, in *any* war.

First to Read Declaration

On July 14, 1776, Isaiah Thomas of Worcester, Massachusetts, became the first person to read the *Declaration of Independence* publicly in Massachusetts.

From 1858 to 1906, Ida Lewis, at left, saved scores of people from drowning and became New England's greatest female lifesaver.

First to Use Bathtub

A reliable source tells us that Eli Whitney, known for his invention of the cotton gin, was the first Yankee to use a bathtub (as we know it today). He imported one from England around 1820.

First to Wear Sideburns

General Ambrose E. Burnside was elected governor of Rhode Island three times, and in 1875 he became a United States senator. But his name is remembered and recorded in our history as the first man to wear and thus popularize sideburns. (Why we don't call them burnsides has us stumped!)

First to Holler "GOLD!"

A Rutland, Vermont, resident named Walter Colton was the first person to make a public announcement of the discovery of gold in California. Unfortunately, he did not become wealthy.

First to Urge Public Education

Horace Mann, born in Franklin, Massachusetts, on May 4, 1796, was more influential in improving the quality of American public education than any other individual. He became first secretary for the Massachusetts Board of Education in 1837, and devoted his life to improving public schools.

First to Receive Social Security

In 1940, at the age of sixty-six, Ida Fuller of Ludlow, Vermont, received the first Social Security check ever issued. The check, dated January 31, 1940, was issued for twenty-two dollars. A native of Vermont all her life, Miss Fuller celebrated her 100th birthday on September 16,1974, and still received her checks.

First Wac

The first woman to enlist in an American army was Deborah Sampson, great-great-granddaughter of William Bradford, who was born in Plympton, Massachusetts, on December 17, 1760. At the age of twenty-one, tired of the drudgery of her life on a farm, she made herself a set of men's clothes, and went to Uxbridge where, on May 23, 1782, she enlisted in the Continental Army. She was attached to Colonel Shepard's 4th Massachusetts Regiment and marched to West Point, where she became "Private Robert Shirtliff" and was outfitted in full army uniform. Despite two wounds, Deborah's secret was not discovered until she became ill during the next year. Dropped from the roll, she arrived home on November 1, 1783, was married two years later, and embarked on a career as a lecturer, sounding what was probably the "first call to American womanhood to take its place in the new liberty." In 1803, Deborah obtained a soldier's pension from Congress. She died in 1827 and is now honored by a monument located at the Rock Ridge Cemetery in Sharon, Massachusetts.

Most Fervent Flag Raiser

Every day of her life, weather and health permitting, from the time she was twenty-two years old, Susie Mae Pettingill of Rockport, Massachusetts, raised and lowered the American flag in the yard on the side of her house. For her grand patriotic spirit she received a personal letter from President Eisenhower in 1960. Susie Mae faithfully tended her flag (replacing it when necessary) for some seventy years. Once, when a storm knocked her pole over, the town gave her a new one. She died in her home in Rockport on May 22, 1966.

Fastest Ice Cream Eater

Bennett DeAngelo, twenty-five, of 42 Westminster Avenue, Watertown, Massachusetts, set a New England record on August 7, 1977, when he ate three pounds, six ounces of ice cream in ninety seconds at the Dean Dairy Ice Cream Parlor in Waltham. (We failed to ask him which flavor tasted *that* good!)

Greatest Contest Winner

Mrs. Gladys Plummer Andersen of Cumberland Center, Maine, won more than 1,600 national contests over a period of years, starting in the 1930s. Mrs. Andersen tells how she got going: "I was sitting in the hammock one day, looking through a farm magazine. A full page ad about 'Hen Pills' that would make hens lay more eggs interested me. I wrote a little jingle about the ad and it sounded so good I decided to send it to the company . . . not for a prize because it wasn't a contest. Soon after, I received two large boxes of hen pills in the mail and a nice letter. That gave me the idea for entering contests where good prizes were given."

Included in the hundreds of prizes she received were refrigerators, radios, television sets, twenty cigarette lighters, freezers and loads of food to fill them, 140 pairs of nylon hosiery, airplane trips, watches, and money. Quaker Oats even sent her and a friend to Miami Beach for a week's vacation.

Mrs. Andersen's largest cash prize was $2,500, which she received for winning a dog food contest.

Greatest Hoaxter

Louis Timothy Stone was a master at testing the gullability of people, and his sharp wit and great sense of humor made him a legend in newspaperdom.

Born in Winsted, Connecticut, in 1876, Stone served for many years as editor of the *Winsted Evening Citizen* until his death in 1933. In the course of his career, he sent a number of fabricated stories out on the national wire, and more often than not, they were picked up and reported as true. His yarns included: the story of the Winsted Wild Man; a bulldog with maternal instincts that hatched and raised a family of chicks; a bald-headed man who had a spider tattooed on top of his head to keep the flies away; and a rattlesnake that bit into a tire by mistake and was blown up. His tale of a trout that grew a fur coat may have been stretching it a bit, but eyewitness accounts confirm that Stone did have a pet trout in his backyard stream that would appear every day when he called to eat a piece of meat off a spoon. . . .

First Human Fly

On a spring day in 1920, George Gibson Polley from Marblehead, Massachusetts, inched his way up the outside of the fifty-seven-story Woolworth Building in New York City, which, at the time, was the tallest building in the United States. When the brave climber reached the thirtieth floor, a police sergeant stuck his head out a window and asked if he had a permit from the city to scale the building. The climber did not, and he was promptly arrested.

Nonetheless, Polley went on to climb an estimated 2,000 buildings, and earn recognition as the country's first "human fly." He conquered such landmarks as the Custom House and Little Building in Boston, the city halls in Lynn and Portland, the tallest hotel in Manchester, New Hampshire, and a department store in Montpelier. (This latter building was only four floors high, but it was the tallest thing in town.) In Hartford, he climbed the sides of three buildings in one day, and in Providence, he shinnied all the way to the top of the tallest flagpole, blindfolded.

"My father was a daredevil, but he never took any unnecessary chances," recalled his son, G. Gibson Polley. "Before he went up the side of a building, he always checked out the exterior to make sure there were no loose bricks, or that the wood hadn't rotted away." He usually wore a white suit and sneakers as he climbed, and if he thought it could be done safely, he would deliberately "slip" and drop a floor to the next ledge below at least once during a climb.

Polley died in 1927 at the age of twenty-nine, not from a fall, but during an operation for a brain tumor.

THE BETTMANN ARCHIVE

First Showman

Phineas Taylor Barnum was born in Bridgeport, Connecticut, on July 5, 1810, and became the first professional showman in the country. Contrary to popular misconception, Barnum did not make his mark with the circus; he did not become involved with the big top until he was sixty years old. Rather, he spent his career getting mass audiences interested in musical concerts and sideshows. His first attraction was Joice Heth, an aged black woman whom he billed as George Washington's 161-year-old nurse. When the venerable lady died, the hoax was exposed. Undoubtedly, Barnum's most famous exhibit centered around the tiny Charles S. Stratton, known as Tom Thumb. Twenty million tickets were sold to people who waited in line for hours to see the famous, twenty-five-inch-tall man who also proved to be Barnum's most profitable investment. (Barnum and Tom Thumb are shown above.)

Greatest Teacher-Magician

Bernard Whitman of the Industrial Arts Department of Weymouth (Massachusetts) Public Schools improved upon many older teaching methods and inspired his students to work on such unusual projects as a one-man submarine, a hovercraft, and an eight-inch Newtonian telescope. But Whitman is a record holder as the only magician in the world to perfect a six-minute act, the late "Great Thurston's" floating ball illusion. In 1961 he was awarded the Gold Cup by the Society of American Magicians for his skill in this act.

Quickest Mathematician

Born in Cabot, Vermont, in 1804, Zerah Colburn was dazzling the scientists of two continents with one of the quickest mathematical minds of his age when he was still a young boy. Answering such complex arithmetic questions as: "How many seconds are there in 2,000 years?" with less than a minute's hesitation, he was exhibited before large audiences in the United States and Europe as one of the wonders of the world. Surprisingly enough, when Zerah grew old enough to desire a more conventional job, he was unsuccessful. He tried teaching, then preaching, then teaching again, but never attained quite the necessary patience or the rudimentary literary skills.

First Mental Hospital

McLean Hospital in Belmont, Massachusetts, was the first mental hospital to open in New England. It admitted the first patient on October 6, 1818.

First Superwoman

Hessie Wanner Donahue kayoed famed fighter John L. Sullivan in a small Arkansas town in March, 1892; she was the only woman ever to accomplish such a feat. Although sparring with Sullivan in the ring as part of a bogus competition to attract crowds, she became angry when the muscle man hit her a little too hard, and forgetting the pretense of their match, she hit back at him, knocking him cold. Hessie was a New Englander from birth, and she died in South Boston in 1961 at the age of eighty-seven.

First Superman

Leo Hyatt, better known as "Superman" Hyatt, was the first and most famous strong man of vaudeville days to come from New England. A native of Syria, Leo spent his boyhood in a gym in Lawrence, Massachusetts, developing his muscles. His show business career was launched in 1920, when he lifted a Studebaker onto his shoulders during a contest.

Hyatt could wrap a steel bar around his arm, pound twentypenny nails into a board with his fist and then pull them out with his teeth, and toss around a 321-pound beer keg filled with bricks. His more unusual stunts separated him from all other muscle men. In one, he would stretch out on a bed of nails, place an anvil on his chest, and invite members of the audience to come and pound on the anvil. He also carried a piano around on the stage, and once acted as the "centerpiece" in a tug of war between a pair of draft horses and a truck. Hyatt later told a reporter that the most difficult part of this latter stunt was the fact that his nose started to tickle, and he didn't have a hand free to scratch it!

First Superman Model

In 1934, Mayo Kaan from Winthrop, Massachusetts, posed for the original Superman comic-book sketches. "I spent about six months posing for those sketches," said Kaan. "They took all sorts of photos, too. I'd hang from wires, and pretend I was flying. I'd stick my chest way out, and pretend bullets were bouncing off it." Following his modeling stint, Mayo returned to Winthrop, and some years later opened a chain of health clubs.

Most Notorious Spy

Benedict Arnold, son of a prominent Rhode Island man, was born in Norwich, Connecticut, on January 14, 1741, and went on to become New England's most notorious spy. In 1778, he was placed in command of the army in Philadelphia, and his love for the fine things in life led him to socialize a bit too much with Loyalists in the city. After a series of reprimands and arrests, he died, not from the gallows as some might think, but from illness, in 1801.

Strongest Man

Elmer Bitgood (also shown on this book's cover), a one-time resident of Voluntown, Connecticut, appears to us to be the strongest man who ever lived in New England. According to an article that appeared in the *Providence Sunday Journal* on February 24, 1946, in his prime Elmer could squat under a table loaded with stone weighing 2,400 pounds, place his hands on a small stool, and with his shoulders and back raise the table three or four inches off the platform. (This must have been the strongest table in New England, even without Elmer.) He could also press a 230-pound dumbbell over his head and hold out at arm's length a rock weighing more than 150 pounds.

At the age of twenty-five, when he weighed 290 pounds, Elmer lifted the front end of a freight car off a track, and offered to put it back for a price. (No dummy, he!) Although he had a right arm like a leg of mutton, Bitgood was never reported to be overly ambitious, and spent most of his time with his almost equally strong brother helping neighbors with odd jobs. He died in 1938.

Smallest Utopian Community

Amos Bronson Alcott (pictured above in his study) and Charles Lane purchased a ninety-acre farm near Harvard, Massachusetts, in 1843, which they optimistically named Fruitlands. Along with their families, the two men set up the smallest Utopian venture in New England. Carrying to an extreme position their effort to break free of society's artificialities and return to a simpler "natural" order, the members gave up alcohol, tobacco, and meat; they refused to enslave animals, and even disdained to wear woolen clothes, and instead wore linen robes.

The community's most radical innovations, however, concerned sex and family life. All of the members belonged to what Bronson Alcott called a "Consociate Family," an affectionate spiritual union which would replace the less spontaneous ties of blood and marriage. When Alcott, acting under Lane's influence, affirmed his renunciation of institutional marriage, Mrs. Alcott threatened to move out, and by January of 1844, the venture was abandoned.

First Utopian Community

New England's first Utopian community was Brook Farm, founded in 1841 in West Roxbury, Massachusetts, (nine miles from Boston) by George Ripley. The Brook Farm Institute of Agriculture and Education, as it was officially designated, survived for six years. Most of the 100-odd members were young (many in their early twenties), unmarried, socially prominent, and troubled about their careers. An impressive number of them achieved renown after their experiment with the community: Nathaniel Hawthorne would emerge from obscurity to become one of the nation's best-known writers; George William Curtis would become editor of *Harper's Weekly*; Charles A. Dana, later editor and owner of the *New York Sun;* John Sullivan Dwight, an important figure in the Boston musical world; and Isaac T. Hecker, the founder of America's first Catholic order, the Paulist Fathers.

Most Radical Republican

Thaddeus Stevens, who was born in Danville, Vermont, in 1792, appears to be outstanding as New England's most radical Republican. Following the Civil War, he voiced his most radical views when he strongly suggested that the southern states be treated as "conquered provinces." He ostracized southern politicians for years, and was the first to call for the impeachment of President Andrew Johnson.

First Male Fire Lookout

William Hilton, a native of Bangor, Maine, was the first person to be employed as a forest fire lookout. His job began in 1905 on Maine's Squaw Mountain, in the first fire lookout station, built by a lumber company from Greenville.

First Female Fire Lookout

To the best of our knowledge, Caroline Parmentier was the first woman in the country to secure a job as a fire lookout. She began work in 1951, atop Vermont's Pico Peak. Required to spend eight months each year on the job, Parmentier not only watched for smoke, but was also responsible for keeping trails clear of fallen trees, and surveying miles of phone cables for signs of damage.

Only Covered-Bridge Builder

Milton Graton of Ashland, New Hampshire, is the only builder of authentic wooden covered bridges in New England. Together with his son, Arnold, Graton has left a trail of restored covered bridges "too numerous to mention" all over New England, mostly in Vermont and New Hampshire. Originally a rigging-and-moving contractor, Graton moved his first bridge in Vermont in 1959 to make room for a road. With each restoration since then, Graton says he has learned something from the old builders, whose work was flawless. In 1969, Graton Associates built its first covered bridge in Woodstock, Vermont; this was the first authentic covered bridge for public use in New England constructed since the turn of the century. (Others may have been built before this, but they were not authentic because of the tons of steel used in their construction.)

Best Bridge Photographer

Edmund Homer Royce of St. Albans, Vermont, started photographing Vermont's covered bridges in 1930, and in his lifetime he took pictures of every bridge standing in the state. To the best of our knowledge, this makes Mr. Royce a first, and an only!

First Kindergarten

Elizabeth Palmer Peabody of Salem, Massachusetts, established the first kindergarten in America. The Pinckney Street Kindergarten in Boston was started in 1861 to set young children in the path of righteousness.

Most Daring Baker

In 1863, when eighteen-year-old Josephine Miller refused to leave her house, even though the Union general told her that it was situated right in the middle of what was about to become the Battle of Gettysburg, she baked batch after batch of good brown bread for the members of the 1st Massachusetts Regiment. Refusing payment for her food, which she dished out for two days as the battle raged around her, she did accept the offer of six soldiers to run back to the 3rd Corps's commissary stores for fresh flour. The men returned with not only flour, but raisins, currants, and a whole sheep — from which, in the words of one account, "a rattling good meal was made." Her efforts as the country's most daring baker were rewarded twenty-five years later, when she was honored at the dedication of the 1st Massachusetts Regiment battle monument in Gettysburg.

First Traffic Regulator

William Eno, who settled in Saugatuck, Connecticut, prepared a brochure called "Rules for Driving" that was endorsed in 1909 as the world's first police traffic regulations. The same year, Eno wrote the first book ever to deal with traffic problems, and became a consultant on the subject to London and Paris.

Oldest Columnist

At ninety-three years of age, Clara Jane Hallett of Hyannis, Massachusetts, was still contributing a weekly column to the *Barnstable Patriot,* making her the oldest columnist in New England. She was affiliated with the *Patriot* for more than fifty years, and we surmise that she also deserves a place in our records as the first and only woman to work for one Cape Cod newspaper for this length of time. Miss Hallet lived to see her 100th birthday, and died on March 28, 1959.

Most Famous Astrologist

Evangeline Adams had a way with reading the stars, and her uncanny accuracy in predicting nationwide disasters made her at one time the most widely-quoted and sought-after astrologist in America. Among her regular customers were J. Pierpont Morgan, Enrico Caruso, Seymour Crowell, president of the New York Stock Exchange, and James J. Hill, the railroad magnate. Miss Adams became interested in astrology while studying at Boston University, and in 1895 she opened an office in Boston's Copley Hotel, casting horoscopes as a means of support. From Boston she went on to New York, where she stated the predictions that made her famous. She foresaw the stock crash of 1929, and in 1930 she declared that World War II would come within fifteen years. She even predicted her own death, which occurred on November 10, 1932.

Oldest Cabbie

In 1972, the late Tony Raneri retired from the cab driving business at the age of eighty-four. He began his taxi driving career in Boston in 1909, and holds a record as the oldest cab driver in the United States.

Courtesy of Florence O'Donnell

GENE DIXON

Most Famous Female Cabbie

Rosie LeCours of Everett, Massachusetts, was one of the first three women in the state to receive a taxi driver's license, and in 1948, when she bought her ownership medallion, we are quite sure she became the first woman in all of New England to own her own cab. "Rosie the Riveter," as she has sometimes been called, became a permanent fixture around Boston's South Station during its heyday, and she shuttled mayors, governors, celebrities, and other VIPs around town. In 1962 she was named Cabbie of the Year. Rosie is still an active cabbie, and she has gotten her hand into politics as well. She was elected the first city counselor of Everett.

Best Moneymaker

John Taber, who lived in Portland, Maine, in the early 1800s, was about the best moneymaker that we have heard tell of. Although financial transactions in Maine at the time were conducted with either Massachusetts currency or solid silver coins, John Taber began to pay his debts with his own hand-signed promissory notes. Since Taber was a very reputable commercial shipper, his notes were highly valued in the community, and as they began to pass from hand to hand they were accepted as legal currency. Unfortunately, when the events leading up to the War of 1812 bankrupted his firm, the very honest Mr. Taber was left with many worthless promissory notes and no silver.

Oldest Firepole Slider

Ben Ellis, born in 1893 in Boston's Back Bay, claims to be the oldest person to still be sliding down a firepole. He still uses the pole to reach the bottom of his three-story place of business — a fire appliance company. Ellis's interest in fires began at an early age; he once jumped out of a classroom window in elementary school to follow a passing horse-drawn engine after his teacher had barred the door to prevent him from chasing it. Since that time, the venerable Ellis has been made honorary chief to so many fire departments, so many times, that he cannot remember the number.

Courtesy of Florence O'Donnell

Oldest Population Records

New Hampshire has maintained the oldest population records of any New England state. They start with 1007.

First Goldfish Gulper

Contrary to popular opinion, the first person to gulp a live goldfish as a college stunt was not Lothrop Withington, Jr., although the Harvard University student's feat in March, 1939, and the resultant publicity in *Life* magazine did start the goldfish gulping craze of the 1930s. The first college goldfish gulping actually occurred in January of 1913, when Frank Farnham Greenleaf of Dartmouth College ate a live goldfish to win a twenty-five cent bet with a classmate.

Spryest Great-Grandmother

Although not a native New Englander, Mrs. Emma Gatewood of Galliopolis, Ohio, set a Yankee record that deserves note. In the fall of 1955, she arrived at the top of Maine's Mount Katahdin, and became the first woman to walk the entire length of the Appalachian Trail from Georgia to Maine. (It goes without saying that she was also the first great-grandmother to accomplish this arduous journey.) And as if this were not enough in itself, Mrs. Gatewood repeated the trek in 1957 . . . another record for the same great-grandmother.

Greatest Vermont Walker

Truman R. Temple spent a great deal of his leisure time walking, and his claim to fame is that he walked in every single town in Vermont. His datebook indicates that he devoted his vacations to journeying, also taking advantage of weekends and holidays and sandwiching in an occasional trip of a day or two. Fit as a fiddle, he lived to be ninety-four.

First to Climb Mount Washington

An Irishman named Darby Field was the first white man to climb Mount Washington, according to our documentation of events in that area. Accompanied by two Indians, he accomplished this task in June of 1642. A monument along Route 16 between Pinkham Notch and Wildcat Ski Area commemorates his feat.

First to Walk Around America

John Krohn, the marathon walker who covered the entire perimeter of the United States on foot, was the first person to complete such a feat. He began his journey on June 1, 1908, and ended it 357 days later. Although other walkers have crossed the country since then, Krohn is the only one we know of who meticulously followed the outer perimeter.

First Pilgrim Baby

Elizabeth Pabodie, the first child born to the first settlers of America, is immortalized by a statue in her honor which stands in the Commons Burial Ground in Little Compton, Rhode Island.

Greatest Birdcarver

Anthony Elmer Crowell was born in East Harwich, Massachusetts, in 1862. He spent all of his life on Cape Cod, and devoted more than forty years to the carving of birds and decoys. A master artist, Crowell drew his birds first, and made his own carving pattern. His birds received two prime coats of paint in thin colors, and then markings were applied a minimum of four or five times. White cedar was used exclusively. First working on ducks and shore birds, Crowell progressed to song birds, and as the years passed, he added further detail to his work, mounting his birds on bases of shells and rocks, most also intricately carved out of wood. When rheumatism in his fingers became so severe that he could not hold a knife tightly enough to carve, Crowell was forced to give up his lifelong work. He died in 1951 at the age of eighty-nine. But his masterpieces have left a notable legacy and his carved birds command prices on the collectors' market into the thousands.

PAUL DARLING

Only Cannon Maker

Al Blair is the only engineer we know of who builds perfect working replicas of American cannons and then sometimes fires them off. An employee of the Bedford Laboratories of Raytheon Company where he labors over more sophisticated missiles, Blair is shown above as he fires his miniature, homemade, twenty-three-pound Long Tom from the front porch of his home in Marshfield, Massachusetts.

Kindest Nurseryman

John Chapman, better known as "Johnny Appleseed," was born in Leominster, Massachusetts, on September 26, 1774. Details concerning his early years are unclear to historians, but the boy lost his mother at the age of two, and at some time moved to Longmeadow. Contrary to popular belief, Johnny was not a scatterer of apple seeds, but rather a practical nurseryman. He planted seeds, set out orchards, and sold or gave trees to the pioneers. One of his nurseries contained 15,000 seedlings. It is believed that Johnny started a westward pilgrimage about 1797 as a self-appointed missionary, sharing the views of Emanuel Swedenborg and the Church of the New Jerusalem. Numerous monuments show the route he followed through the midwest, doing what he could to help other people, and making peace between the Indians and the settlers. He died in Fort Wayne, Indiana, on March 18, 1845.

Courtesy of Mrs. Evelyn B. Hachey

Greatest Family Tree

On November 19, 1667, in New Haven, Connecticut, Richard Edwards of Hartford married Elizabeth Tuthill (later spelled Tuttle), an Englishwoman. Although the couple had only one son and four daughters, the family tree that was rooted with their marriage had a noteworthy influence on the culture and history of America. By 1900, there were more than 1,400 descendents of Richard and Elizabeth Edwards; among them were 100 clergymen (including Jonathan Edwards), more than 100 lawyers, 295 college graduates, sixty-five college professors, thirteen college presidents, sixty doctors, sixty prominent authors, seventy-five military officers, eighty public officials, thirty judges, senators, governors, foreign ministers, and a President of the United States — Ulysses S. Grant. Pretty good support for theories of heredity and genetics!

Courtesy of Charlotte McCartney

Only Woman to Found a City

Elizabeth Pole, daughter of Sir William Pole of Devonshire, England, came to America when she was forty-five years old. Settling first in Dorchester, she decided to look for more land, and set out on foot one day from Boston to see what she could find. As the story goes, Elizabeth drove her cattle through the woods until she reached an area known as Tetiquet (now East Taunton). Here, in 1637, she traded a jackknife and a pack of beans with three Indians for a portion of their woodlands. A year later, forty-six people, including her brother, bought a sixty-four square mile plantation called Cohannet from Chief Massasoit for two shillings per acre. Elizabeth's name was not on the list of original purchasers of the land that in time became known as Taunton, but Myles Standish and his company credited her as the founder of the town. Taunton became a city in 1864, and is the only city in America to be founded by a woman.

First Antislavery Speech

John Dickson, born in Keene, New Hampshire, made the first antislavery speech in Congress in 1835.

Greatest Female Lifesaver

Ida Walley Zoradia Lewis deserves a place in history as New England's greatest salt-water heroine. From 1858 to 1906 she saved some forty people from drowning in the choppy, stormy seas off Newport, Rhode Island.

Born on February 25, 1842, Ida spent her early childhood on Lime Rock, an island 250 yards from Newport's mainland, where her father served as keeper of the light. Every day she would row to Newport for groceries and to take her brothers and sisters to school. People who knew her claimed that this boat-handling experience gave her the strength necessary for the outstanding feats she later performed.

Her first rescue was on a September afternoon in 1858, when four boys cruising near Lime Rock overturned a skiff. Ida spotted them floundering in the water and saved all four.

As time went by, Ida used her wits and muscles to save more endangered sailors. Practicing the technique taught by her father to prevent her boat from overturning, she would grab the drowning person by the arm, give a backward heave on an oar, and pull the victim in. If in bad shape, she would take them to the lighthouse* for dry clothes.

By 1867, at the age of twenty-five, Ida had saved ten people in nine years. After she rescued two drowning soldiers, New York City newspapers spread her story, and she became a national figure. Statesmen, military, and naval leaders flocked to visit this famous woman on her lonely perch in the ocean. But Ida remained deaf to the praise, simply contending that she was only doing her job.

Commercially-minded businessmen marketed Ida Lewis hats and scarfs, the Ida Lewis waltz became popular, and marriage proposals poured in. With her national recognition at its peak, Ida was offered $1,500 a month to go on stage, but she refused. In 1869 she welcomed 9,000 uninvited visitors, including Admiral George Dewey, General William T. Sherman, Susan B. Anthony, and Vice President Schuyler Colfax. She received many awards for her valor, and the federal government established a special citation for lifesavers and made Ida the first recipient.

Despite her rise to fame, Ida Lewis lived a quiet life, carrying on her father's task of keeping the light. She died on October 24, 1911, at the age of sixty-nine.

Courtesy of Norris Randolph

**The lighthouse was later renamed the Ida Lewis Yacht Club, making it the only club of its kind in the United States named for a woman . . . another record worth noting.*

Greatest Male Lifesaver

Captain Joshua James of Hull, Massachusetts, performed more courageous lifesaving acts than any other person in New England history. When his mother and sister drowned in a boat accident in 1836, ten-year-old Joshua decided to dedicate his life to preventing more unnecessary deaths. He saved a total of 626 lives in his career.

Only Grandmother Lobsterwoman

Lobstering may seem like an odd profession for most women, but not for Elsie Ilvonen of South Thomaston, Maine, who is one of the very few full-time lobsterwomen in New England, and, as far as we can tell, the only grandmother who works the traps all year. In business since 1964, Elsie sometimes works with her husband Carl, but prefers to set and haul her traps independently. Elsie has seven children and eleven grandchildren, and enjoys touring the countryside by motorcycle in her spare time. When asked when she will retire, Elsie replied, "You only retire from a job. Old lobster people never die, they just cut back."

Least Remembered Heroine

Dorothea Lynde Dix, the great nineteenth-century crusader for the rights and humane treatment of the mentally ill, is probably New England's least remembered heroine. Although she was responsible for the institution of more than 100 hospitals and asylums in her forty years of reform work, she is scarcely mentioned in history books and her grave near Boston bears neither epitaph nor date.

First Department-Store Santa

Although he never realized that he was launching an American tradition, James Edgar of Brockton, Massachusetts, was the very first department-store Santa Claus. Owner of the Boston Store, Edgar was always fond of wearing costumes, and at Christmastime in 1890, he decided to come to work dressed as Santa. People brought their children from miles around to see this marvel, and as word spread, so too did the popularity of Santas in other stores across the nation.

Most Fearless Frontiersman

John Capen Adams, born in Medway, Massachusetts, on October 22, 1812, was better known by his nickname, "Grizzly." In 1849 he headed west, and started a collection of living wild animals that became world famous. In the process, Grizzly was pawed, chawed, charged, tossed, and trampled by every conceivable animal of the western plains and mountains.

In the spring of 1860, Adams met with P.T. Barnum and worked out a deal with the circusman for continued exhibition of his collection, which included several grizzly bears.* At the time of their meeting, Adams removed his hat and showed Barnum a blow he had received en route from "General Fremont," one of his prize bears. "His skull was literally broken in," wrote Barnum in his memoirs. "It had on various occasions been struck by the fearful paws of his grizzly students; and the last blow . . . had opened his brain so the workings were visible!"

After several months of failing health following this injury, Grizzly Adams retired to Neponset, Massachusetts, where he died on October 25, 1860.

*One of the grizzlies, Sampson, holds a record of his own. He was the largest grizzly ever captured, tipping the scale at three-quarters of a ton!

Most Professional Storyteller

John J. Cronan instituted story telling in public libraries in 1911, and continued to amaze and delight his audiences for almost fifty years. Often accompanied and aided by his wife Mary, Cronan was able to completely enchant anyone within earshot, and he was featured in a story in the *Saturday Evening Post*. In a busy period, the Cronans would host as many as ninety-eight story hours per month, for groups of children at the Boston Public Library and branches.

Nantucket's Last Indian

A French painter named Hermione Dassel created this portrait of Abram Api Quarry, the last native Indian to live on Nantucket. Sole survivor of the once powerful Wampanoag tribe, Abram refused to wear shoes for his sitting, much to the artist's dismay. At her insistence, he brought a pair along, but told her that she'd have to paint them off his feet, and under the table. (Note that's exactly where they are!) Abram died on November 25, 1854, at the age of eighty-two. His body lies in an unmarked grave on the island, which he called Nauticon.

Greatest Necromaniac

Frances B. Hiller, who lived in Wilmington, Massachusetts, in the mid 1800s, was the greatest necromaniac we have ever heard of. She and her husband had drawn up the plans for their own caskets long before their deaths, and after her husband had departed, Mrs. Hiller took to lying in her own, which was displayed in the front parlor of her home. Eventually she had a wax model of herself made, which she attired in her splendid burial robes and set into the coffin. The robes were made of corded silk, trimmed with 500 yards of handmade silk lace which had been embroidered in France; they cost over $20,000.

The casket, an exact duplicate of her husband's, stood five feet from the floor, weighed over 2,000 pounds, and took a woodcarver three-and-a-half years to build. Made of four-inch thick mahogany, the cover had intricate carvings of ivy vines, a skull with a lizard creeping out of one eye socket, an owl holding a field mouse in his talons, and a covey of angels, serpents, bats, cupids, and dragons. Inside the outer box, which was supported by eight heavy brass lion's paws, was an inner chamber, covered over with gold and silver plates engraved with portraits of the Hillers and their twenty-three children who had all died as infants. A metal hammock was suspended from the four corners of the inner chamber, and it was on this hammock that Mrs. Hiller lay.

To hold the two caskets, Mrs. Hiller had a mausoleum built. It was forty feet square and forty feet high, with plate glass windows behind a bronze grating; two guards were stationed day and night and a light was kept burning at all times. Thirty-five years after Mrs. Hiller passed away, the townspeople who lived near Wildwood Cemetery agreed that the huge mausoleum was an eyesore. The building was razed, and the Hillers' caskets were lowered into the ground, where they are marked only by two stone urns over simple bronze plaques. But the strange woman who was so intrigued with thoughts of death lives on as a one-of-a-kind New Englander.

Courtesy of John Mason

First to Lay Cable

Cyrus Field, of Stockbridge, Massachusetts, laid the first transatlantic cable, from Ireland to Newfoundland, in 1866. When he first conceived of the idea in the mid 1850s, Field consulted telegraph experts to determine that such a long cable would work, then he set out to raise money for the venture. He and four friends sought funding through America and England, finally managing to procure $1,750,000.

It took a London firm six months to make the 2,500 miles of cable, which was composed of a copper core with gutta-percha insulation, wrapped in rope, with an outer armament of iron wire. Its bulk and weight were so great that no single existing ship could carry it, so a plan was devised to distribute the cable from two ships. The American frigate *Niagara,* after laying half the cable, would rendezvous with the British warship *Agamemnon* in mid ocean to pick up the rest. After a grand send-off, Field shipped out aboard the *Niagara,* never knowing what adventures lay in store.

Five days out, a brakeman checked the line rather abruptly and the cable snapped. Dismayed as he watched a half million dollars sink to the floor of the ocean, Field returned to Ireland. After a year of more fund raising and alterations on the cable's brake mechanism, Field started off again with a new plan. This time the ships would make the splice in mid ocean *before* laying out the cable, and the line would be fed out slowly from both ends. The ships survived a violent storm, made the splice, and started laying cable, but when they were three miles apart the cable snapped and broke off the *Niagara's* stern. They met again, started off again, and got eighty miles before the cable snapped. So they met again, tried once more, and since they were over 100 miles apart when the cable went dead, both ships returned, downhearted, to London.

Undaunted, Field set out a week later for his third attempt with both ships. The rendezvous was successful, the splice was made, and after several weeks of smooth sailing, Field reached Newfoundland. The celebrations that August of 1858 were phenomenal. Yet in the midst of a celebratory banquet, word reached Field that the cable had gone dead, having snapped in mid ocean.

In 1865, a British firm offered to supply new cable, and the *Great Eastern,* the largest sailing ship in the world, which had been built since Field's last attempt, was made available. The *Great Eastern* could hold all the cable herself, so the problems of coordinating two ships could be avoided. Field, the only American still working on the venture, set sail in June, 1865, along with 5,000 tons of new cable. But tiny bits of wire were found protruding through the cable's casing, allowing current to escape into the ocean. Strained by being continually hauled up for repairs, the cable snapped when the ship was only 600 miles from Newfoundland.

Field set out from Ireland on the *Great Eastern* for his fifth attempt, with his undying optimism as evident as ever. The journey was relatively uneventful, smooth sailing all the way, and on July 28, 1866, Cyrus Field did reach Newfoundland, minus the welcoming committee, with the first successful transatlantic cable still intact.

Courtesy of Samuel Carter III

THE GALLERY COLLECTIONS

Smallest Sisters

The famous "Fairy Sisters," Cissie and Victoria Foster, who toured the United States fascinating thousands in the 1870s, were the smallest people in New England; they were said to be smaller than even General Tom Thumb (another New Englander). Cissie Foster, the older, at ten years of age weighed only twelve pounds and had grown to her full height of twenty-one inches. The sisters were promoted by a man whose office was located in the old State House in Boston.

Most Determined Sisters

Five eccentric young women, the Smith sisters, joined hands around their family's kitchen table in the early 1800s and vowed never to wed. Named Hancy Zephina, Cyrinthea Lucretia, Laurilla Aleroyla, Julia Evalina, and Abby Hadassah, they dressed exactly alike, and were a very talented group.

Laurilla and Abby taught music, Julia translated the Bible five times (twice from Greek, twice from Hebrew, and once from Latin)*, Cyrinthea was an accomplished portrait painter, and Hancy designed a log cabin and built a boat that she sailed on the Connecticut River.

In 1873, Julia and Abby, the last two living Smith sisters, asked to be permitted to vote for town officers in Glastonbury. Their request was denied, so the sisters planned for revenge. When the tax collector showed up to collect for their farm, they refused to pay. Officials came and took their seven cows away to auction off for the debt; the sisters attended the auction, bought back their cows, and continued this practice for many years, never admitting to paying their taxes in such a backward town!

Courtesy of Mary Lou Kitsen

Most Medical Family

The most medical family in all of New England, to our way of thinking, is the "Bonesetter Sweets" who have lived in Rhode Island since John Sweet came to the state from Salem, Massachusetts, in 1637. Although family members were usually employed as artisans — stonemasons, blacksmiths, wheelwrights, and carpenters — every generation had at least one man trained in the avocation of bonesetting, and the practitioners' success in treating all sorts of fractures, sprains, and dislocations led to theories of a magical power passed down through the family. With the emergence of stricter regulations on practicing physicians, the Sweet family became known less as mystical healers than competent doctors; descendents still practice orthopedic medicine in Rhode Island.

**Julia was the first woman to translate the Bible!*

Most Famous Nurse

Clara Barton was born in North Oxford, Massachusetts, in 1830. As a young woman, she took a job copying patents in Washington, D.C., and here learned of the horrible suffering of wounded men left unattended on the battlefields of the Civil War. She launched a campaign to remedy their suffering, and traveled through Massachusetts begging money and supplies. Gathering blankets, food, clothing, and medicine, she returned to Washington and persistently begged permission to go to the battlefront. Given consent, she first went to Culpepper, Virginia, to lend her help. The loaded wagons were ready and her corps of women were waiting. She said afterward that all she had to do when she finally got the major's permission was to take the hoop out of her skirt, climb onto a wagon, and start.

Among the wounded soldiers that she nursed was Jules Gulay from Switzerland, who invited her to visit his parents in Geneva. It was on this visit abroad that she learned about the effective Red Cross in Europe. Following earnest fund raising and meetings in Washington upon her return, she organized the first chapter of the American Red Cross in 1881. Clara Barton became the first president, and served with the organization for the remaining twenty-four years of her life, accepting a final assignment as a nurse in Turkey at the age of seventy-five.

McLEAN HOSPITAL

First Male Nurses

McLean Hospital was the first in the country to accept and train male nurses. The class of 1888 contained fifteen women and five men, the first trained graduate male nurses. Pictured here, they were, left to right, Robert E. Crulman, Henry B. Northrop, Frank Livingston, Byron Atwood, and George B. Ober.

First Female Nurse

On September 1, 1872, Linda Richards enrolled in a pilot class with five other women in the first American training school, at the Hospital for Women and Children, in Boston. At the end of the year-long course, four of the five young women had yet to make up for sick time, and Richards was the only one to receive a diploma, thus becoming the first professional, trained nurse. She devoted her life to people, and died on April 16, 1930.

Greatest Historian

Although some critics thought his writing left something to be desired, Francis Parkman deserves note as New England's greatest nineteenth-century historian. Born in Boston on September 16, 1823, Parkman wrote many books on both domestic and foreign events. Able to extract the drama out of history, he once remarked that pretty girls and horses were the "first-ratest things in nature." Parkman died on November 8, 1893.

Greatest Headmaster

Frank Learoyd Boyden spent sixty-six years as a prep school headmaster, and by the time he stepped down from his post at Deerfield Academy in 1968, he had been honored by four US presidents, showered with honorary degrees, and revered by hundreds of men who were once his "boys." Author John McPhee wrote Boyden's biography, *The Headmaster,* and attested to his eminence, calling him "one of the greatest headmasters in history."

Boyden's reign was the longest of any headmaster in New England. He retired at the age of eighty-eight, and died on April 25, 1972, at ninety-three.

Longest Term as Teacher

Caroline Ardelia Yale, a relative of Elihu Yale who founded the university that bears his name, was born in Charlotte, Vermont, in 1848, and served more years at one school than any other teacher we know of in New England. In 1870, she was invited to join the teaching staff at the Clarke School for the Deaf in Northampton, Massachusetts, and she stayed on for sixty-three years.

Shortest Term as President

Urian Oakes served the shortest term as a college president when, in 1672, he acted in that capacity just long enough to preside over commencement exercises at Harvard University.

Harvard's First Woman Professor

Dr. Helen Maud Cam of Cambridge, England, was Harvard's first full-fledged female professor. An authority on English constitutional history, she taught in the history department from 1948 to 1954.

MACY LAWRENCE

Oldest College Student

In 1953, after fifty-seven years in the food and produce business, Morris Springer retired at the urging of his sons. The next two months were the most tiresome experience of his life, so he said later, and he decided to go back to school. After graduating from grammar school in 1955 as class valedictorian, and from high school as class president four years later, he entered Boston University in 1959 at the age of eighty-seven on a four-year evening scholarship, becoming the oldest college student in New England, and quite possibly, the world.

Oldest Military Company

The Ancient and Honorable Artillery Company of Massachusetts is the oldest chartered military company in the United States, and the third oldest military organization in the western world. The group was founded by Robert Keayne, who brought the tradition with him from England, in 1637. Although members of the unit have fought in every American war from Myles Standish's Indian skirmishes to the Vietnam conflict, the unit has never faced battle as its own entity. Indeed, it might be said that the Ancient and Honorable Artillery Company has created the ideal military life. Instead of long marches, KP, and armed combat, the outfit enjoys banquets, toasts, speeches, parades, traditions, and "tours of duty."

In 1974, the Ancients became the first foreign military group ever to parade through the streets of Moscow, as they completed their 337th Annual Fall Field Day Tour of Duty in Russia. The company's mission was to march in full uniform through Red Square to the Kremlin, and lay a wreath at the Tomb of the Unknown Soldier. As guests of General Pavel Batov, head of the Soviet War Veterans, the Ancients were wined and dined at a postparade reception at the Hotel Metropol. The smiling Russian officers offered toasts to a tradition dating back to William Dawes and General George Lincoln, famed revolutionaries of the American past. And after swapping dollars for rubles to shop for souvenirs, the Ancients entertained the elite of the Russian armed forces and the United States Embassy at a formal banquet. Robert L. Marr, captain of the Ancient and Honorables, presented General Batov with a New England-made, gold-plated Colt .45. The general, according to reports, was very moved.

But the Ancient and Honorables march at home, too. Best known in Boston for their annual parade on the first Monday in June from Faneuil Hall to the State House, and on up to the Old South Church where a wreath is laid on the grave of Robert Keayne, the company drills in their historic quarters atop Faneuil Hall and in Boston's Armory.

Courtesy of Jack Drummey

Most Fervent Evangelist

William Miller, a Massachusetts soldier-turned-evangelist, incited thousands of New Englanders with prophesies of the final Judgement Day. Shortly after receiving his first message from God in 1831, he was offered a preaching position in Dresden, and ecstatically began to prepare his sermon. Before the final Judgement Day came, Miller said, there would be four definite signs. Wonders would be seen in the skies,the earth would tremble, there would be a war among mankind, and man would show marked intelligence in earthly progress. As if by divine power, the signs began to appear: on November 13, 1833, thousands of stars were seen falling from the skies, and balls of fire blazed in the heavens for fifty minutes; earthquakes were reported in England, India, and the West Indies; numerous revolutions began to break out in Europe; and Miller's generation became aware of their unprecedented creative and industrial expansion.

Such awesome prophesies won Miller many disciples, but the message became twisted over the years. By the time Miller set a date for the end of the world (April 3, 1843), he was well on his way to insanity and his following had grown into a hysterical movement, more caught up in the drama of the event than in the meaning. Gathering on hilltops in preparation for the Last Judgement, Millerites sang, chanted, and burned their earthly possessions in huge bonfires.

When April 3 came and went without the world ending, Miller corrected the prophesy to March 21, 1844. As the new Judgement Day approached, the cult ceased burying their dead; the bodies were carried to camps so they might all ascend into Heaven together. Again the fateful day came and went without the expected holocaust, and Miller once again set the date at October 23, 1844. The intact dawn of October 24 brought mass suicides and hysterical rages of disillusioned followers. William Miller, having neglected to give away all his vast earthly fortunes, lived for five more years on a luxurious farm, and then died, completely insane, in 1849.

Courtesy of M. Robert Beasley

RICHARD W. GREEN

Oldest Employee

When John Hannafin retired from the E.T. Wright Shoe Company in Rockland, Massachusetts, in September of 1977, he set a record as being the oldest continuous employee of any one company in New England, and we'd guess, in all the country. Hannafin began working for the company when he was fourteen years old, and after seventy-six years of service, he left at the age of ninety. To our way of thinking, he deserves a mighty big gold watch! And if his loyalty to the shoe business wasn't enough, Hannafin has also received an award for being the oldest member of the Fraternal Order of Eagles in New England.

Oldest Men's Club

The Old Men's Club, shown here at their annual meeting at Lake Compounce Park, in Bristol, Connecticut, has just about the oldest members we have ever seen!

MALCOLM TAYLOR

Last Hurdy-Gurdy Man

Marino Persechini, now of West Roxbury, Massachusetts, was Boston's (and all of New England's) last hurdy-gurdy man. Born on April 19, 1880, on a boat outside New York Harbor, he was taken back to Italy by his parents at the age of two, but returned to America in 1906. For $155, a fortune in those days, he bought the hurdy-gurdy that would be with him for years, a lute-shaped instrument that he transported on a pushcart, always adorned with a small American flag and seasonal garlands.

Marino would begin his stroll at 9 AM, making the rounds of Boston's downtown streets, usually working until 7 PM. He was a familiar sight around Boylston, Washington, and Arlington streets, especially on Filene's corner. He featured old-time favorites like "Beer Barrel Polka" and "Deep Purple" as he turned the crank at a steady rhythm, and bragged to friends that he never missed a beat.

When he first began his career, there were other hurdy-gurdy men, but as the years wore on, especially during the last twenty-five of the seventy-five years he worked, his competition faded into oblivion. Finally, at the persistent urging of his family, when he was ninety-three, Marino sold his cherished companion to Frank O'Boy, president of Towne Antiques in Brookline Village, for $5,000, with the understanding that he would retain visiting rights. More than 200 friends, relatives, neighbors, and shopkeepers gathered to pay tribute to the maestro on the day of the sale. Boston's Mayor Kevin White declared a "Marino Persechini Day," and presented him with a gold pin shaped like Faneuil Hall's famous grasshopper. But the highlight of the party occurred when it came time to turn over the key. The last of Boston's street troubadors just couldn't resist cranking out a few more tunes and he immediately swung into "My Wild Irish Rose."

In 1977, Marino celebrated his ninety-seventh birthday, and his granddaughter reported to us at press time that he was "fit as a fiddle and still smiling."

Courtesy of Florence O'Donnell

PAUL DARLING

Most Famous Cardiologist

Paul Dudley White, best known for his promotion of exercise as a method of warding off heart disease, was New England's most famous cardiologist. Shown here in a familiar pose aboard the bicycle he rode until the end of his life, he utilized every available opportunity to educate both the lay public and fellow physicians to the preventative value of controlled diet and exercise.

In 1914, when cardiology was still scoffed at by most physicians as a "paltry specialty," White imported one of America's first electrocardiographs to the Massachusetts General Hospital. He later established the hospital's famous cardiac unit, and was one of the original founders of the American Medical Association. Always mindful of his role as a physician, White liked to spend one-third of his time conducting new research (his scientific curiosity never ceased to amaze his colleagues), one-third in patient care (his patients included President Eisenhower and Pablo Casals),one-third in teaching, reading, and writing (White published more than 700 scientific papers in his career, and his early book *Heart Disease* became one of the definitive works on the subject). He was felled by a stroke in 1973, at the age of eighty-seven.

First MIT Woman

Ellen H. Swallow enrolled in 1871 to study chemistry at MIT and became the first woman to attend the Institute. At the time, the faculty was faced with a dilemma: it was generally assumed that the school was only for men, but the charter had not excluded women. MIT accepted Miss Swallow as a special student, charging her no tuition fees and not entering her on their records, figuring she would not attend classes for very long. Much to their amazement, Miss Swallow was successful in completing the course and was awarded a Bachelor of Science degree in 1873.

Only Bald Head Club

Founded in 1911, New England's first, and to our knowledge, only Bald Head Club was started in Falls Village, Connecticut. A three-inch bald spot qualified anybody and once a member, the purpose was to laugh at being hairless. Annual dues were one dollar per year and anyone using a restorative was immediately expelled.

Only Ostrich Murderer

The only man in New England history convicted of murdering an ostrich lived in Boston, Massachusetts. Known locally as Mr. Nemo, he was slightly inebriated on the night of April 9, 1926, when he attempted to break into what he thought was the back door to his house. He had, instead, scaled the wall surrounding the Franklin Park Zoo and broken through the door of the ostrich pen. The ostrich, a very surprised 250-pound bird known as George Washington, attempted to peck the intruder to death, and Mr. Nemo, never totally aware of what he was doing, strangled the animal.

Only Man Buried in Two States

Sam Jones, a carpenter, has the distinction of being the only New Englander to be buried in two separate towns. When he lost a leg working at his trade in Washington, New Hampshire, it was buried there with the dignified inscription: "Here lies the leg of Samuel Jones, 1846." When the rest of him died a few years later, he was buried in Massachusetts.

7
Politics and Punishments

Only Oyster Stew Murder
On March 26, 1860, Warren Gibbs died in Pelham, Massachusetts. His wife was accused by the deceased man's brother of killing her husband by sprinkling arsenic in his oyster stew. As far as we know, this is the only case of willful oyster stew murder in New England.

Most Famous Murder Case
Lizzie Borden, a thirty-two year old woman from Fall River, Massachusetts, was accused of murdering her father and stepmother with an ax on August 4, 1892. Her trial, which lasted thirteen days, attracted nationwide attention, and she was acquitted on June 20, 1893. She has since been featured in ballads and rhymes, and her trial was the first case to make front page newspaper news.

Most Controversial Trial
The world-famous trial of Sacco and Vanzetti was held in 1921 in the Norfolk County Courthouse in Dedham, Massachusetts. Accused of robbing and murdering a paymaster and guard in Braintree a year before, the two immigrants' political views probably figured into the trial as much as their supposed crime. The men were declared guilty and later executed, but the storm of controversy as to their guilt or innocence rages on.

Last Woman Whipped in Public
We don't know the victim's name, but Stone No. 6 at old Newfane Hill, Vermont, marks the spot where, in 1805, the last woman was whipped in public.

New England's first women's movement rallied for suffrage. At left are some staunch suffragists who got their way in 1920.

Only Woman Pirate to Hang
Rachel Wall, the only woman pirate in history to be hanged, met her death from the gallows in 1789 for stealing a hat. The place of the hanging was not recorded, but it occurred in Massachusetts.

Last Pregnant Woman Hanged
On July 2, 1778, Bathsheba Spooner was hanged in Worcester, Massachusetts, for the murder of her husband. With child at the time, she became the last pregnant woman to be hanged in the state. (Accomplices in the crime included three other men who were also executed, making Mr. Spooner's murder the first and last crime in Massachusetts to lead to the execution of four people — five counting the unborn child — for the same crime.

Largest Crowd at a Hanging
Grim and grizzly as the story is, we can note that the Jason Fairbanks murder case in Dedham, Massachusetts, attracted the largest crowd of followers of any crime at the time, and the convicted man's hanging on September 10, 1801, was witnessed by more people than any other public hanging. Historians estimate that 10,000 people showed up to watch Fairbanks swing, with 711 carriages making the trip from Boston. Fairbanks was accused of the murder of Elizabeth Fales, his sweetheart, who was found stabbed to death on May 18, 1801.

Last Pirate Hanged in Boston
A Mexican pirate named Ruiz was hanged at the Leverett Street jail in Boston in September, 1835. He was the last pirate to be executed in the city of Boston, as of this book's press date.

New Hampshire's Last Hanging

On May 6, 1868, Samuel Mills was hanged in North Haverhill, New Hampshire, an event that became the state's last public hanging. Mills worked as a laborer for George Maxwell, an aged farmer in Franconia. Learning that his employer had sold his farm for $3,000, Mills decided to steal the money. He assaulted Maxwell with an ax and killed him, but failed to find the money. After the crime he left the state, but was tracked down by Boston detective Moses Sargent, who found the criminal in a copper mine in Illinois.

Maine's Last Hanging

The last lynching in Maine occurred in April, 1873. When Sheriff Hayden and two deputies set off in pursuit of Jim Cullen, the town brute who had stolen a pair of boots from David Dudley's store, Cullen shot the sheriff, sparing several witnesses. Once Cullen was later apprehended, the town's people were anxious to see him hang. A hooded mob seized the transport that was taking him to the Presque Isle jail and carried out their own execution, hanging the culprit from the nearest maple tree.

Courtesy of Jim Barrows and Oscar Nedlar

Boston's First Irish Policeman

Boston's first Irish policeman was Barney McGinniskin from County Cork, who was appointed to the force by Mayor John Prescott Bigelow in 1851 in hopes of winning the immigrant vote. Police commissioner Francis Tukey strongly objected but McGinniskin overcame all objections and served three years before being fired in 1854. He died in 1868 at the age of sixty-two and is buried at St. Augustines Cemetery in South Boston.

Lynn's First Policeman

William Waite, six feet tall and 225 pounds, was sworn in as the first police officer in Lynn, Massachusetts, on May 14, 1850. In-between arrests, Waite worked in the community as a butcher.

Only Police-Manned Airport

Logan Airport in Boston is the only airport in the United States that is manned by state police. Troof F is in charge there.

First To Use CB

State Trooper Francis McVeigh of Company A on the Massachusetts Turnpike in Weston is credited as being the first New England "Smokey with Ears," and was responsible for the widespread popularity of the CB in relation to law enforcement. Trooper McVeigh began using a CB in his cruiser in 1974 and kept a daily log to prove to his superiors the advantage of being able to communicate with the motorists. As a result, in 1975, he and his fellow officers received full consent and approval for the use of CB in police work.

Courtesy of Florence O'Donnell

First Fiction Libel Suit

A novel entitled *Cape Cod Folks,* published in 1881, became the first work of fiction in the United States to be the occasion of a libel suit. The book's author, Sally Pratt McLean, gave her characters the names of living people whom she had known in a section of Plymouth, Massachusetts. Lorenzo Leonard Nightengale so resented the use of his name that he brought suit against the publishers, A. Williams and Company, to the tune of $10,000. It is believed that every person whose name appeared in the novel was given some kind of compensation from the chagrined publisher, varying from $150 to fifty cents. Nightengale was awarded $1,095.

First Book Banned in Boston

The first book ever banned in Boston was the novel *The Woman Who Did,* written by Grant Allen in 1894. Ironically, the book was conceived as ammunition in the crusade against prostitution, but the Boston Public Library refused to permit the book onto its shelves, nevertheless. The city did not appoint its first official censor until 1904, when Mayor Patrick A. Collins chose John M. Casey for the post. Some of the other literature not fit for Boston consumption included Ernest Hemingway's *A Farewell to Arms,* Theodore Dreiser's *An American Tragedy,* and Voltaire's *Candide.* Even the cinema was not safe: *Gone With the Wind* was banned in 1939 because of Clark Gable's last line, and Walt Disney's *Snow White and the Seven Dwarfs* was censored for a ditty sung by Sneezy!

Strongest Beard Supporter

In 1830, when he inherited an old farm in Notown (an unreclaimed gore of land between Leominster and Fitchburg, Massachusetts), bearded Joseph Palmer became the butt of persecution, simply because he refused to surrender to custom when the beard lost favor with the common people. Small boys threw stones at him, women sniffed and crossed the street when they saw him coming, windows in his modest home were broken, and grown men jeered at him. Joe withstood the petty insults until two occurrences.

One Sunday, while kneeling for communion in church, he was ignored by the official clergyman. Deeply offended, Joe strode to the communion table, lifted the cup to his lips and took a drink.

A few days later, as he was coming out of the old Fitchburg Hotel, he was seized by four men armed with shears, brush, soap, and razor. Telling him it was the town sentiment to shave his beard, they flung Joe to the ground, injuring his head. Joe fought back, cutting two of his assailants seriously enough to discourage any further barber work.

But Joe was arrested and charged with "unprovoked assault" on the townsmen. He refused to pay the fine and was locked in the Worcester city jail. Even there he had to fight with his jailors to keep his whiskers. From jail, Joe wrote letters explaining his persecution which were published in the *Worcester Spy*. Other papers picked up the story, and soon people all over Massachusetts raised a clamor.

The authorities realized they could not make a case stick, and Joe was freed. Soon after his release from jail, he moved to Fruitlands, where he hoped to practice many of his social reforms. Although the experimental community failed, Joe stayed on, and lived to see the beard again take its place of honor on noted Americans. He died on October 30, 1875, at the age of eighty-four. A simple monument to him in the cemetery in North Leominster bears a carving of Joe's head with his noble beard etched in marble, and a simple legend: "Persecuted for Wearing a Beard."

Courtesy of John Mason

First Liquor Law

A law requiring a permit for the sale of spirits was passed in Massachusetts in 1633. This legislation appears to be the first regulating alcoholic beverages.

First Prohibition State

In 1851, the Maine legislature enacted into law "An act for the Suppression of Drinking Houses and Tippling Shops." This law prohibited the manufacture and sale of any intoxicating liquors in the state, and made Maine the first in the country to pass prohibition.

First Driver's License Law

For the first time in 1899, the city of Boston passed an ordinance requiring all drivers to be licensed. As far as we can tell, this was the first law of its kind.

First to be Caught for Speeding

In 1904, as he was chauffeuring a foreign limousine for a resident of Newport, Rhode Island, Michael Woods was apprehended by a policeman on a bicycle, who charged that the automobile was "driving faster than a horse could trot." He was fined fifteen dollars, plus two dollars and sixty cents for court costs, and became the first motorist in New England history to be stopped for speeding.

First Speed Law

Alarmed by the potential hazards of fast-moving vehicles, in 1901 Connecticut passed the world's first automobile speed law: twelve miles per hour within city limits; fifteen miles per hour in rural areas.

First License Plates

In 1903, Massachusetts became the first state in New England to require registration plates. Frederick Tudor of Brookline was issued Plate No. 1 that same year.

First Woman Driver

Records pertaining to the first licensed drivers in New England are a little hazy, but our research seems to indicate that the region's first licensed woman driver was Anne T. Knotts of Jamaica Plain, Massachusetts, who received license permit No. 102 from the Boston Park Department in 1900.

Youngest Licensed Driver

At the age of eleven years and thirty days, in 1904 Edward Esty of Brookline, Massachusetts, was granted a chauffeur's license, and became New England's youngest licensed driver. Prior to 1907, no test was generally required to obtain a driver's license. There was no set age limit and many thirteen and fourteen-year-old youths were granted restricted licenses (driving under parental guidance), which posed a problem for authorities. Finally, as a result of young Esty's application, the Highway Commission deemed it necessary to design a test. Esty passed the sixteen-minute exam with flying colors, much to the surprise of the authorities. In 1907, a more restrictive test was required to obtain a chauffeur's license. It was not until the early 1920s that a test was required for a private operator's license.

Courtesy of Eugene A. Barile

Hardest Laws to Obey

Massachusetts law still requires all bearded men to pay a "goatee" tax, and you can't eat peanuts in church or use tomatoes in your clam chowder. Boston hotel proprietors must still provide "bed 'n board" for a guest's horse, but you must never wash an animal, vehicle, or shake a mat or carpet in any street. No ringing of church bells, or any bells, on account of illness, if forbidden by the Board of Health.

You must not ride or drive your jackass or beast of burden at speeds greater than seven miles per hour. (It was once illegal for Bostonians to own a dog larger than ten inches high.) In Quincy, Massachusetts, roller skating along any city street is forbidden, and another ordinance implies that only an officer of the law may spy on others. Also, "No person shall expose himself to the sun while bathing in any creek, road, or other public waterway within the (Quincy) city limits." A Boston law forbids swimming, or bathing, in waters surrounding, or within the city, in view of any dwelling.

Contrary to the mandatory one-year sentence that is part of the Massachusetts gun law, another Quincy law states that "Every man must escort his family to church carrying a musket." In Springfield, Massachusetts, you may not sell buttermilk on Sunday, but you may still graze your cow on the Boston Common. Before taking a wife, a man who lives in Truro, Massachusetts, must kill six birds or three blackbirds. If a Connecticut beau writes love notes to a girl his mother forbids him to see, he could be arrested. To lure bees away from their keeper is also a criminal act in Connecticut. In Portland, Maine, it is against the law to tickle a girl under the chin with a feather duster. And to walk, or jog, down any street in Maine with untied shoe laces is illegal. To blow one's nose in public in Waterville, Maine, could command a jail sentence.

When two motorists meet at a highway intersection in New Hampshire, the law states that each must remain stationary until the other has gone. Before taking a bath in Maryville, Vermont, one must get a permit from the Board of Selectmen. A hen must not appear in a matinee in Coddle, Vermont, and the law requires that all carriage wheels must be constructed entirely from lampwicks. It is also illegal to whistle underwater in any pond or lake in Vermont.

Courtesy of Florence O'Donnell

First Free Public School

In January of 1645, the townspeople of Dedham, Massachusetts, resolved to raise twenty pounds per annum to maintain a schoolmaster for the education of their children. Although other school buildings had been built prior to this date, Dedham stands on record as the first place in the country to support a free public school through public taxation.

First Integrated School

The first integrated school in the United States was opened by Nat Allen on January 4, 1854, in West Newton, Massachusetts. There were thirty-eight students in the first class.

First Free Haven for Religion

In 1636, Roger Williams founded Rhode Island as the first free haven of religious worship in America.

First Free Republic

On May 4, 1776, two months before the other twelve colonies officially stated their position, the General Assembly of the Colony of Rhode Island formally declared its independence from Great Britain. This brave act made the state the first free republic of America.

Smallest and Last Republic

Way up north in New England, a handful of people got together in the early 1800s and formed the smallest republic ever organized in New England. By 1824, approximately 300 people were living on old Indian hunting lands along the New Hampshire and Canadian borders. British and American commissioners found themselves in an awkward situation, unable to agree on the boundary line between the two countries. When New Hampshire claimed the territory, the Indian Stream people objected; when Canada made moves to take it over, they protested this also.

The inhabitants of Indian Stream would have nothing to do with either side. In the summer of 1832, they met at the Centre Schoolhouse and set up their republic. It was all very simple. The entire voting population, with each person representing his own interests, made up the legislative body, and the supreme court, or Council of Five, acted as the executive department. Trial by jury was provided and a military company of forty men was formed for protection against "foreign invasion." In addition to taxes on land, buildings, and livestock to pay for schools and roads, Indian Stream had a poll tax on all male citizens, excluding ministers, paupers, and idiots. That year the new republic elected three judges, seven sextons, three fence viewers, and a sheriff, who inverted a huge potash kettle on a flat rock to serve as a jail.

Neither the United States nor Canada took immediate notice of the new republic, and for a time the government functioned effectively. But eventually, "treason krept in" and it became difficult for the republic to enforce its own laws. When New Hampshire officials began to get nosy, the republic's president asked the US Attorney General for an opinion stating that Indian Stream was under the jurisdiction of the federal government, but not that of New Hampshire. The reply came back, saying "If you are within the limits of this government, it is because you are within the limits of the State of New Hampshire." Trouble started immediately, and the boundary dispute between New Hampshire and Canada flared up once again. After several outbreaks, New Hampshire militia came to spend the winter in Indian Stream, and the Indian Stream people realized the state meant business.

In 1840, the Indian Stream Republic disappeared forever from the map, and the town of Pittsburg, New Hampshire, took its place.

Courtesy of Kevin Aylmer and Roger Bowen

First Gerrymanderer

In 1812, Governor Elbridge Gerry from Marblehead, Massachusetts, went as far as he could to obtain additional Senate seats for republicans who would oppose the federalists. He redistricted his territory in Essex County so that it resembled a salamander, and from that day forward was credited as the first to practice a political trick today called gerrymandering.

STEPHEN T. WHITNEY

Most Predictable Elections

Taylor City doesn't appear on any road map, but it is a very real place, and the seat for the least democratic, most predictable elections in New England. Made up of the Taylor families living in Parsonfield, Maine, and South Effingham, New Hampshire, the town's history dates back to the early 1800s.

In 1950, G. Earl Taylor decided to run as the first mayor of this familial community. Even though he had an opponent, he won easily, since the entire population of Taylor City is made up of Taylors. Since that time, an election for mayor has been held every year, on the eve of July 4. Bribery is part of the deal, and children are given popsicles in exchange for their votes.

One year, the election almost went awry, and it appeared that a non-Taylor was gaining support. But two young Taylor voters put firecrackers in the ballot box and blew it up; the election went unanimously to the incumbent Taylor mayor. And with tactics like this, we assume a Taylor will be in power for many more years to come!

Courtesy of Audry Lynch

First to Secede from Union

Muscongus, a small island off the coast of Maine, seceded from the United States in 1860, and became the first area to leave the Union. Being such a small community, the rest of the nation never took notice and only the town of Bristol became directly involved in this action. It all began when Maine first joined the Union. A geodesic survey was made of the coast and somehow, inadvertently, Muscongus was left off the map. At first, this hardly upset the fishing community on the island. Their livelihood came from the sea and happenings on the main land were of little consequence to them; they paid their taxes and that was that.

But as time went on, the island people gradually wanted more say in the affairs of the town. Described as a "tough lot," the fishermen rowed across the bay to cast their ballots and the town of Bristol took heed of their arrival. A totally democratic community landing in republican Bristol usually found several brawls before the day was over.

But the Lincoln-Douglas election of 1860 finally pushed the Muscongusites into seceding from the nation. Their numbers had grown large enough by this year to significantly influence Bristol's ballot box. And, when it became apparent that Bristol, Maine, would go democratic for the first time in history as a result of the Muscongus voters, the town and state officials were stunned and became hesitant to announce the results. Someone discovered that Muscongus was not on the map, and declared the islanders' ballots invalid.

The anger felt by the islanders reflects in the action they took upon hearing about their invalidation. Voting to secede, they set up their own government and a state of normalcy returned. Maine refused to recognize the secession and continued to send the tax collector and the draft agent to the island. But these officials got nowhere and often had to flee from the tough, rifle-bearing fishermen who greeted them. It was not until 1934 that the Muscongusites petitioned the federal government to accept their island as part of the United States of America, once again.

Only Vermonter to be President

Calvin Coolidge was born in Plymouth, Vermont, on July 4, 1872*, and to this date, he is the only native Vermonter to become a United States president. Following the death of President Harding, Coolidge was sworn into office on August 3, 1923, by his seventy-eight year old father, a notary public. The ceremony was held by candlelight in the farmhouse where he grew up; this event by itself marks the only time a president was sworn into office in Vermont, and the only time, as far as we can tell, that a father officiated at such a ceremony for his own son. Later Coolidge set another record when he became the first president to talk on the radio.

A Man of Three Firsts

Matthew Lyon, an emigrant from Ireland who settled in Connecticut upon arriving in this country, is the first, and thus far only, person to have been elected to Congress by three states — Vermont, Kentucky, and Arkansas.

He also stands on record for another first which occurred on October 4, 1796, when he was arrested for his criticism of President Adams, and became the first person indicted under the Alien and Sedition laws. Sentenced to four months in prison at Vergennes, Vermont, and fined $1,000, the incarcerated Lyon was reelected to the House of Representatives by his Vermont constituents, becoming the first politician to be reelected to office while in jail.

Oldest Capitol with Legislature Meeting in Same Chambers

The New Hampshire State House in Concord, built from 1816 to 1819, is the oldest state capitol in the country in which the legislature still meets in its original chambers. The building itself has been enlarged several times since the Civil War because its legislature is another record holder — with as many as 400 members, it is the largest state legislative body in the United States.

**To date, Coolidge is the only United States president born on the Fourth of July — a record for him and for his mother!*

First Place to Vote

The tiny mountain town of Dixville Notch, New Hampshire, is the first place in the United States to cast its votes in a presidential election. The polls open at one minute past midnight, but since the town population is so small, they close about fifteen minutes later.

Greatest Female Bill Passer

Mary Ginn Worthley was the first woman ever to present a major bill before the Maine Legislature, and she is a record holder in this book for getting a bill passed in every session of the legislature from 1947 to 1972!

First Woman State House Speaker

Mrs. Consuelo Northrop Bailey from South Burlington, Vermont, was the first woman to be elected speaker of a state House of Representatives. She was elected to this position in the Vermont House in 1953, and served the regular term of two years.

LAWRENCE F. WILLARD

Oldest Town Hall in Use

The town hall in Pelham, Massachusetts, is New England's oldest town hall in continuous use. The first town meeting was held here in 1743 and special meetings are scheduled each year to keep the tradition — and the record — going.

First Urban Renewal

The market complex at Faneuil Hall, currently called Faneuil Hall Marketplace, is cited by city planners as America's first example of urban renewal. This distinction has been so given because the three market buildings were initiated by city government using reclaimed land. They were designed by Alexander Parris and built in 1826 under Mayor Josiah Quincy.

Largest Collection of Memorabilia

J. Doyle DeWitt, former president of Travelers Insurance Companies, put together the largest private collection of American political memorabilia ever assembled. DeWitt started to collect political items, mostly from presidential campaigns, in the 1920s when they were cheap and easily available. When he died in 1972 at the age of seventy, his collection totaled 40,000 pieces of anything that had to do with American politics — buttons, bows, banners, song sheets, broadsides, campaign literature, photographs, paintings, china, silverware, pencils, parasols, and paperweights.

Courtesy of Bill Ryan

Greatest Real Estate Deal

In 1685, an Indian sachem named Wonalanset transacted New England's greatest real estate deal with a family named Usher. According to the terms of the deal, he gave the Ushers the right to the mines, minerals, and ores within the limits of New Hampshire, and the Indian reserved one quarter of the ores and one seventeenth of the baser minerals for his own use.

Only Privately Owned Common

The Weston Green in Weston, Vermont, is the only public common in New England which is owned by a private group rather than by the town. In this case the group is an organization of nine women who call themselves the Farrar Park Association. Named after the Farrar family who donated the land for the purpose, the organization has been responsible for the maintenance of the common since its origin in 1870.

Only Town to Own Another Town's Common

Fitzwilliam, New Hampshire, is the only town in New England that ever owned the common of another town. Once a part of Fitzwilliam, Troy became an independent town in 1855, but it did not receive the title to its common from Fitzwilliam until 1894. (Whether Fitzwilliam was holding out for a reason, or whether it just kept sloppy records, we don't know for sure.)

Last of the GAR

Although once a popular organization in this country, by 1927 the Grand Army of the Republic had dwindled to a handful of men. Without dispute, the last true soldier of this army was Commander A.E. Lincoln, who continued to hold meetings of the GAR Post in Kingston, Massachusetts, even when he was the sole surviving member. Dressed in full uniform and displaying the company's flag before an assembly of vacant chairs, Lincoln called the role, served as chaplain, adjutant, and sergeant at arms before a group of his comrades that was present only in spirit. For months, Lincoln continued the meetings until his death in 1931.

First Flag Under Fire

The town flag of Bedford, Massachusetts, earned the honor of being the first flag to come under fire in the American Revolution. It was carried by the Bedford Minute Men when they rushed to the aid of their neighbors in the town of Concord on April 19, 1775.

First Purple Heart(s)

Three men from Connecticut — Daniel Bissell, Daniel Brown, and Elijah Churchill — were the first three men in history to receive the Purple Heart award. The honor was instituted by George Washington on August 7, 1782, and presented to the men on May 9, 1783.

GREAT DEBATE

First Offensive Action in American Revolution?

New Hampshire's Claim

In 1774, Paul Revere brought news to Portsmouth that the British were planning to remove the cannon, shot, and powder from Fort William and Mary in New Castle, New Hampshire. In December of that year, patriots from Portsmouth, Exeter, and New Castle stormed the fort and captured it. The powder and shot were removed to Exeter and transported across the country to be used eventually against the British at Bunker Hill.

There is nothing at all questionable or unclear about the action or the date of the action here in New Castle. It was not only the first offensive action, but it was the first military action of any kind in the American Revolution.

Courtesy of John D. Swanson

Vermont's Claim

According to the *Encyclopaedia Britannica* and all accepted histories, the American Revolution did not officially start until April 19, 1775. Therefore, Ethan Allen's aggressive action in rowing across Lake Champlain and capturing Fort Ticonderoga on May 10, 1775, less than a month after the official start of this war, was and must remain the first offensive action of the American Revolution.

Courtesy of Vrest Orton

Massachusetts' Claim

Though the following may not be considered a military act, the first armed resistance to the British rule took place in Great Barrington, Massachusetts, on August 16, 1774, when about 500 armed men stopped the King's judges from holding court there.

Courtesy of Horace H. Turner

Connecticut's Claim

The Green Mountain Boys were led by Ethan Allen and his brother and Remember Baker aided him. These three men came from Litchfield, Connecticut. So, I feel, Connecticut deserves the credit for being the first to show offensive action during the Revolution.

Courtesy of Mrs. W.A. Dower

Rhode Island's Claim

When our neighbors usurp our claim to having taken the first offensive action against the British, it is necessary for us to rise up and sink them as we did *HMS Gaspee* on June 9, 1772.

The armed British schooner *Gaspee* blockaded the shipping lanes into Providence in order to collect taxes on sugar and rum. This caused commerce to be reduced and resulted in unemployment and wide-spread hatred for England, taxes, and the *Gaspee*. When the American ship *Hannah* was being chased, her captain lured the *Gaspee* into waters so shallow that she ran aground and was stuck there until high tide next morning. Some patriots at Sabin's saloon planned a surprise attack on the stranded ship. In eight longboats they rowed to the ship (near Pawtuxet), shot the captain, overpowered the *Gaspee,* and set the hated ship on fire. Undoubtedly the first offensive action against the British.

Courtesy of Calvin B. Dewey

We have yet to hear from Maine, but we're going to stop now before we start another Revolution!

8

Creative Achievements

First Bible

Printed by Samuel Kneeland and Timothy Green in Boston in the mid 1700s, the country's first Bible written in English was published for Daniel Henchman.

First Book

In 1640, the first book ever published in America was printed by Stephen Daye at Harvard College in Cambridge, Massachusetts. When the first edition came out, it was commonly known as *The Psalms in Metre, Faithfully translated for the Use, Edification, and Comfort of the Saints in Publick and Private, especially in New England.*

First Almanac

The first almanac ever printed in this country was *The Freeman's Oath,* published at Harvard College in Cambridge, Massachusetts, in 1639.

First Self History

When William Chauncey Fowler's book, *History of Durham, 1662-1866,* was published with funds appropriated at a town meeting, Durham, Connecticut, became the first town to publish its own history at its own expense.

Oldest Publication

The Old Farmer's Almanac(k), started in 1792 by Robert B. Thomas of West Boylston, Massachusetts, is the country's oldest continuous publication. Its famous long-range weather forecasts have been accurate eighty percent of the time.

Alexander Calder's Stegosaurus, *shown at left, stands in downtown Hartford. It may well be New England's most controversial sculpture.*

First Cookbook

America's first cookbook, written by Amelia Simmons and published by Hudson and Goodwin in Hartford, Connecticut, in 1796, carried the unpretentious title of *American Cookery or the art of Dressing Viands, Fish, Poultry & Vegetables and the best Modes of Making Pastes, Puffs, Pies, Tarts, Puddings Custards & Preserves and All Kinds of Cakes from the Imperial Plumb to Plain Cake adapted to This Country & All grades of Life.*

Best-Selling Cookbook

First published in 1896, *The Boston Cooking School Cookbook* has become America's best-selling cookbook. When Fannie Farmer brought her creation to Little, Brown & Company in Boston to have it published, they agreed only on the stipulation that she cover the initial printing costs herself. The last thing the country needed, they said, was another women's recipe book.

First Science Fiction Writer

Planning moon shots long before the development of space centers, John L. Riddell, a New England resident, was America's first writer of space travel science fiction stories. Riddell's first space story concerning a lunar shot was written in 1847, two decades before Jules Verne wrote of similar happenings.

First Poetess

Anne Bradstreet, a cultivated English woman who married and moved to the American colonies, was the first American poetess. She lived and wrote in Boston, Massachusetts, in the 1600s.

First to Translate Heidi

The first English translation of *Heidi* was written by Louise Brooks, a resident of West Medford, Massachusetts. Having spent several years in Germany, Brooks began to translate her favorite German story into English for her children. The first edition of the resultant book was published by Cupples, Upham, & Company of Boston, in 1884.

GREAT DEBATE

Real Mother Goose?

Any self-respecting historian of Boston, Massachusetts, will tell you that the real Mother Goose was born in Boston in 1665, that she really did raise sixteen children, and that the entertaining verses she gurgled to her first grandchild were written down and published by her son-in-law, Thomas Fleet, around 1720, under the title *Songs For The Nursery* or, *Tales From Mother Goose*. On the other hand, any British authority will tell you that Mother Goose rhymes originated in Elizabethan times in England, some as a result of Queen Elizabeth herself. French authorities will tell you that the fables date back to Perrault, a seventeenth-century poet who wrote *Contes de Ma Mere L'Oye*. And any classics scholar will tell you that Aristotle is supposed to have quoted an ancient version of *Hiccory, Diccory, Dock*. Nevertheless, there is a grave in the Old Granary Burying Ground in Boston, near the Paul Revere monument, occupied by none other than the Boston Mother Goose, and it is the first story that we choose to believe!

Only Mountain Newspaper

Issued twice daily throughout the summer from its inception in 1877 until its death by fire in 1907, *Among the Clouds* was the only newspaper printed on the summit of any mountain in the world, and, to the best of our knowledge, its record still stands. Housed in the Summit House on top of Mt. Washington in New Hampshire, *Among the Clouds* was the brainchild of Henry M. Burt, an old-time newspaperman from Springfield, Massachusetts, who billed it as New England's oldest summer resort newspaper.

Oldest Newspaper

The Hartford Courant, started as *The Connecticut Courant* by Thomas Green in Hartford, Connecticut, in 1764, is undisputably the oldest American newspaper still being published.

GREAT DEBATE

First Newspaper?

Claimed by some sources to have been the first newspaper in America, *Publick Occurences Both Foreign and Domestick* was published by Benjamin Harris in the London Coffee House in Boston, Massachusetts, in 1690. This paper, however, had a short life as a result of its inflammatory political statements and its lack of a required license.

Many people therefore claim that the next paper to appear, *The Boston News-Letter,* printed by Bartholomew Green for John Campbell, the postmaster, was the first true American newspaper, having appeared in April of 1704.

Yet another source believes the first truly successful American newspaper was the *New England Courant,* started by James Franklin (older brother to Benjamin) in Boston on August 21, 1721.

Sweetest Revere Bell

The bell that Paul Revere recast in 1816 from an older metal bell and considered his sweetest still tolls in the King's Chapel steeple in Boston, Massachusetts. One of Revere's earliest and largest, the bell weighs two and a half tons.

First Notable Composer

In 1770, when William Billings of Boston, Massachusetts, put aside his tanning trade to open a music shop and publish the *New England Psalm Singer,* he became America's first native composer of any note.

Only Composer to Receive Medal

George M. Cohan, a legend in the field of American songwriting, is the only composer to ever receive a Congressional Medal. Born in Providence, Rhode Island, on July 3, 1878, Cohan was awarded the honor for his patriotic songs "Over There" and "You're a Grand Old Flag."

First Female Player at BSO

In 1952, Doriot Anthony, an accomplished flutist, was chosen to succeed George Laurent, thus becoming the first woman musician ever appointed as a principal player for the Boston Symphony Orchestra.

First Jingle Bells

Although it was published anonymously for many years, the light tune "Jingle Bells" was composed by James Pierpont, a resident of West Medford, Massachusetts, who played it for the first time in 1850 on Mrs. Mary Gleason Waterman's piano. Pierpont, unfortunately, was never able to make his living from his music, and died before "Jingle Bells" was an essential part of American music.

First We Three Kings

"We Three Kings"the popular Christmas carol, is not of old English origin, as many people seem to think. The song was composed by the Reverend Dr. John Henry Hopkins, Jr., a native Vermonter, in 1857.

First to Sing Sweet Adeline

Harold W. Castner of Damariscotta, Maine, was the first person in the world to sing the well-known love ballad "Sweet Adeline" Composed by Harry Armstrong and Richard H. Gerard, the song's "test run" was performed in an elaborate minstrel show in Damariscotta in 1903, when Castner was a young boy.

First Advertised Concert

The first "publicly announced" concert in America was advertised in 1731 in Boston. It featured local musicians.

First Dance Festival

Originating in 1932, Jacob's Pillow was America's first dance festival. And, since it is still held every summer in the township of Becket, Massachusetts, this festival is also America's oldest.

Oldest Band in Vermont

The Grafton Band of Grafton, Vermont, organized in 1867, is the oldest established band in the state.

PETER C. ADAMS

Oldest Drum Band

Organized in 1767, the Mattatuck Drum Band of Waterbury, Connecticut, is the country's oldest drum band in continuous active service. Unlike other old musical groups whose activity has dwindled, the Mattatuck Drum Band has grown continually stronger in membership and enthusiasm over the years.

GREAT DEBATE

Best National Anthem?

The Star-Spangled Banner has been the country's national anthem since 1931, with a 1798 tune and lyrics that date back to 1814. Yet many people have felt over the years that the anthem's imagery, its glorification of war, and its difficult tune make it undesirable as a symbol of our country. While the legislative battle to change the national anthem rages in Washington, D.C., the New England citizens are joining forces to decide the issue at home. Mrs. Julie Rosegrant, of Putney, Vermont, initiated a local campaign in March, 1977, to make *America the Beautiful* the new national anthem, because its emphasis on brotherhood, conservation, and beauty seem more appropriate to the true spirit of America. In defense of the old traditions, two Putney men have formed the Committee to Save Our National Anthem, saying that changing symbols erodes our basic way of life. Still, no one on the committee claims to be able to hit the top notes of "the rockets' red glare" very well . . .

Only Abenaki Art

The only known artwork of the Abenaki Indians is a mysterious petroglyph carved into a rock in Embden, Maine. Authorities disagree on whether the unusual carvings represent a map, a religious shrine, or the story of a battle.

First to Paint Presidents

Gilbert Stuart, born in Saunderstown, Rhode Island, in 1755, was the first artist to paint American presidents. Washington, Adams, Jefferson, Madison, and Monroe sat for him, but his most famous painting, a first of its own accord,was of George Washington.

Longest Painting

America's longest painting, Benjamin Russell's *Panorama of a Whaling Voyage Around the World,* is 1,375 feet long. The painting, portions of which are on display in the Whaling Museum of New Bedford, Massachusetts, depicts a voyage which crossed all seven seas.

Most Elaborate Barn Paintings

The most elaborate paintings on the side of a barn that we have ever heard of were created in Kirby, Vermont, in the early 1900s. Russell Risley, who spent his entire life on a farm in Kirby, occupied his spare time painting friends, neighbors, and nationally-famous people on the side of his weatherbeaten barn. Although the paintings were reputedly lifelike, no one saved any of the artwork when the building fell in the 1940s.

Largest Mural

Cape Cinema in Dennis, Massachusetts, houses the largest single mural in the world. Covering 6,400 square feet of canvas, the oil painting, created by Rockwell Kent and Jo Mielziner, was commissioned by Raymond Moore in 1930.

Greatest Miniature Painting

The question of greatness in art becomes a tricky one, but we'd like to stick our necks out anyway and say that the most famous miniature painting in New England is Edward Malbone's *The Hours,* created in 1801. Three figures painted on ivory represent the past, the present, and the future. The work is six-by-seven inches, and is currently on exhibit at the Providence Atheneum in Providence, Rhode Island.

VINCE MECCA

Most Patriotic Painting

Shown above is one rendering of Archibald M. Willard's *Spirit of '76*, which displays America's Revolutionary zeal better than any other painting we have seen. Willard created fourteen "Spirit" paintings, all remarkably similar, but with enough subtle distinctions to inspire heated controversy over which version was, in fact, the first. Although its claim to being the original rendering has been challenged by several noted authorities, the *Spirit of '76* that hangs in Abbott Hall in Marblehead, Massachusetts, is without a doubt the most famous.

First Instant Photos of Yachts

The first instantaneous photographs of international yacht races were taken by Edward Hale Lincoln in 1866, using only a horse blanket thrown over the lens instead of a shutter or filter. Achieving fame for his magnificent flower photography, Lincoln spent the last fifty years of his life in Pittsfield, Massachusetts.

S.R. GILCREAST, JR.

Most Popular Landscape

Commonly known as "Motif Number 1," the fishing shack on the harbor of Rockport, Massachusetts, is the most popular single landscape for New England painters and photographers.

Oldest Skylighted Art Gallery

The Athenaeum in St. Johnsbury, Vermont, an old red brick Victorian building, has a skylighted art gallery considered to be the oldest of its kind in its original form. The gallery features a huge Albert Bierstadt painting, *Domes of the Yosemite,* and includes many other vintage works of art.

Only Public Rockwell Gallery

Old Corner House in Stockbridge, Massachusetts, displays the only collection of Norman Rockwell paintings on display for the public to see.

Largest Hardy Collection

The world's largest collection of works by English author Thomas Hardy is the Hardy Collection at the Colby College Library in Waterville, Maine. Famous for his works *Far from the Madding Crowd* and *The Return of the Native* among others, Hardy found his most receptive audience, surprisingly enough, in New England at the turn of the century.

Best Lincoln Collection

Brown University's John Hay Library in Providence, Rhode Island, features the world's most comprehensive collection of Abraham Lincoln memorabilia.

Largest Monet Collection

America's largest collection of Monet paintings is housed in the Museum of Fine Arts in Boston, Massachusetts. The only larger collection of Monet's work hangs in Paris.

Finest Asiatic Collection

The finest collection of Asiatic art in New England, and probably in the entire country, is displayed in the Museum of Fine Arts in Boston.

Finest New Worldania Collection

Brown University's John Carter Brown Library in Providence, Rhode Island, contains the world's finest collection of maps, manuscripts, and books pertaining to the development of America during the colonial times.

Largest Egyptian Collection

The Museum of Fine Arts in Boston contains the largest collection of Egyptian art outside of Cairo.

Best Arctic Collection

Part of the Dartmouth College Library, the Stefansson Collection on the Polar Region is the country's most extensive collection of arctic works. Tracing the historical exploration of the northern regions primarily through books, pamphlets, and manuscripts, the collection is the culmination of the lifetime work of Dr. Vilhjamur Stefansson, who, until his death in 1962, was the world's leading authority on the arctic zone.

Largest Armor Collection

The John Woodman Higgins Armory in Worcester, Massachusetts, contains the largest private collection of armor on the North American continent. The collection features 157 complete suits of armor and approximately 8,000 other items.

Oldest Museum

The Peabody Museum in Salem, Massachusetts, is the oldest continually operated museum in America. Its first collections were founded by the Salem East India Museum Society in 1799, and moved to the present building in 1824.

Only Stamp Museum

As far as we can tell, the Cardinal Spellman Philatelic Museum in Weston, Massachusetts, is the only postage stamp museum in New England. We do know for sure that it is the only such museum to be awarded full accreditation by the American Association of Museums.

Most American Englishman

The model for the famous *Minute Man* statue on the Battle Green in Lexington, Massachusetts, was actually an Englishman. Although his name is not indicated anywhere except in the town records, Arthur G. Mather posed for eleven months around the turn of the century for the artist, H.H. Kitson.

Most Patriotic Face

Ralph S. Cline of Spruce Head, Maine, who posed in his World War I uniform in 1964 for Andrew Wyeth's famous painting *The Patriot,* must have had the most patriotic face in all of New England.

Most Famous Postmarks

Prior to 1890 (when the federal government took over the job), local postmasters were responsible for creating their own postmarks, and the most famous and perhaps the most original of all of them were John W. Hill's postmarks from Waterbury, Connecticut. Hill's postmarks varied with the season, from a heart around Valentine's Day to a baseball when Waterbury won an important game, to an elephant when the traveling circus came to town.

Most Controversial Sculpture

The Calder *Stegosaurus,* constructed in downtown Hartford, Connecticut, in 1975, is by all of our accounts the most controversial sculpture in New England. The piece, commissioned by the trustees of the Ella Murr McManus Fund, was approved by Hartford city officials in its initial planning stages, but when the final product was erected in Atheneum Square just outside the windows of the mayor's office, the same officials immediately protested the fact that the sculpture simply didn't fit in with the area's staid Greek and Roman Renaissance architecture. The sculpture, however, was part of Hartford's revitalization program, initiated in an attempt to remove that very same staid, dull image of the city. Calder's *Stegosaurus* still presides over Atheneum Square today.

Largest Matchstick Sculpture

Earl Walsh's *City of Religion* sculpture stands four feet high in places, is thirty-two feet long, weighs approximately 400 pounds, and is composed entirely of matchsticks. The work, a replica of a full-fledged city complete with towers, memorial gardens, fountains, and more than a dozen religious temples, took the Haverhill, Massachusetts, resident forty-two years to complete.

Only Official Tree Map

In 1976, Ray Napolitano of Newton, Massachusetts, created a map of the United States by cutting the shape of each state from a chunk of that state's own official tree. It is, to the best of our knowledge, the only such map in existence in the country.

First Gibson Girl

Josephine Gibson Knowlton, youngest sister and constant companion of the famous Charles Dana Gibson, posed for her brother's drawings from childhood on, and served as the original model for his "Gibson Girl" sketches that became world famous in the late 1800s.

BOB HOWARD

Only Mushroom Sculptor

Maria Maravigna of Winchester, Massachusetts, is internationally known for being the only hand sculptor in the world to create mushrooms in minute scientific and botanical detail and color. A portrait painter and artist by trade, she applies her expertise to her mushroom knowledge and has turned out at least 3,000 species.

9
Sports and Games

First Ski Resort

Peckett's of Sugar Hill, New Hampshire, became known as the country's first ski resort and the home of the country's first ski school when Katherine Peckett returned from Switzerland and Austria in 1930 with new ideas for winter sports. The resort became famous, but was unable to compete with the newer facilities and closed its doors in 1967.

First Ski Tow

In a meadow behind Clinton Gilbert's barn in Woodstock, Vermont, is the site of the first ski tow in the United States. In January, 1934, the tow was made from a rope and powered by a Model T Ford engine. It hauled skiers to the top of the mountain, giving birth to skiing in the United States as we know it today.

Longest Ski Lift

Killington Ski Area in Killington, Vermont, boasts that it has the world's longest ski lift. The lift is three-and-one-half-miles long and carries skiers in four-passenger gondolas to Killington Peak, a 3,000-foot vertical rise.

First Skier up Mount Washington

While a student at Dartmouth College in Hanover, New Hampshire, Carl E. Shumway skied to the top of Mount Washington. This historic ascent took place in the winter of 1913. Shumway later went on to be the first to conquer Mount Monadnock on skis on February 22, 1925.

David Geer, pictured at left, has won five world woodchopping competitions, and wields the fastest ax in New England.

Best Nordic Skier

At the 1976 Olympics in Innesbruck, Austria, an American won a silver medal in cross-country skiing competition for the first time in Olympic history. Twenty-year-old Bill Koch of Guilford, Vermont, crossed the finish line second in the thirty-kilometer race. Americans have never been taken seriously as contenders for this grueling type of race. Prior to Koch's record, the best American skier finished fifteenth at the Lake Placid games of 1932.

First Ice Skating Champion

On February 15, 1953, in Davos, Switzerland, Tenley Albright from Newton Center, Massachusetts, became the first United States skater to win the World Figure Skating Championship. She also won the unanimous vote of seven judges — the first time this was ever achieved. Miss Albright was seventeen years old at the time of her triumph.

First Roller Skating Champion

W.H. Fuller of Boston, Massachusetts, was the first champion on roller skates. Fuller met James Plimpton in New York City while ice skating in Central Park and soon entered into a business partnership with the mechanical genius who invented the roller skate. Fuller sold thousands of Plimpton's skates by performing for prospective buyers who presumed they could move as gracefully on the skates as Fuller. He traveled throughout Europe and Asia, staging shows for kings, pharaohs, and various heads of state. His skill was indeed appreciated for many in his audiences had never heard of the strange rolling gadgets.

First Tennis Champion

In 1881, Richard Dudley Sears of Boston, Massachusetts, won the first National Men's Singles Championship, held at the newly built Newport Casino in Newport, Rhode Island.

First Olympic Champion

James Brendan Connolly of South Boston, Massachusetts, was the first person in the world to win an Olympic contest after the games were revived in modern times. In 1896, Connolly went to Greece to join the American team, and won the first event, the Triple Jump. Unfortunately, he was expelled from Harvard University for making the trip.

First Heavyweight Championship

The first heavyweight boxing championship was fought by Abington, Massachusetts, resident John L. Sullivan when he battled against James J. Corbett in 1892. Sullivan became the most famous New England pugilist, winning twelve of his thirty-seven fights by knock-outs!

Youngest to Win World Titles

Lou (Larraping) Brouillard, Hingham resident trained at Joe Beston's Gym in Quincy, Massachusetts, won two world boxing titles before reaching the age of twenty-one. He won the welterweight title from Jack Thompson at Boston Garden in 1930. When he lost that title soon after, he went for the middleweight crown which he won that same year in a seven-round knock-out of Ben Jeby at Polo Grounds in New York.

Best Boxing Column

"Ringside" appears in five national and international publications which makes it the most widely read (and we think the best) boxing column in the world. It is written by Don (Sailor) Sauer of Kingston, Massachusetts.

Oldest Pro Tennis Tournament

The US Pro, the longest-running professional tournament in the tennis world, began in New York City in 1927. The tournament is now held at the Longwood Tennis Club located in Chestnut Hill, Massachusetts.

First Davis Cup Tournament

America's first Davis Cup tennis match, named after Dwight Davis, was held at Davis's home club, the Longwood Tennis Club, in Boston, Massachusetts, on August 8, 1900. A large crowd attended.

Only Tennis Hall of Fame

The National Tennis Hall of Fame and Tennis Museum was established in the old Newport Casino on Bellevue Avenue in Newport, Rhode Island, in 1952. The sport first gained national prestige from the early championships held at the Casino, and the collection of memorabilia and early equipment is the only one of its kind in New England.

Best Baseball Player

New England's best baseball player, Napolean Lajoie, the "Bonaparte of the Batsmen," was born in Woonsocket, Rhode Island, on September 5, 1875, and played primarily with the Cleveland American League Club. A terrific hitter, he was one of the few players in baseball history to have made more than 3,000 hits. But Lajoie earned his title not only by grandslams; he could handle any team position well.

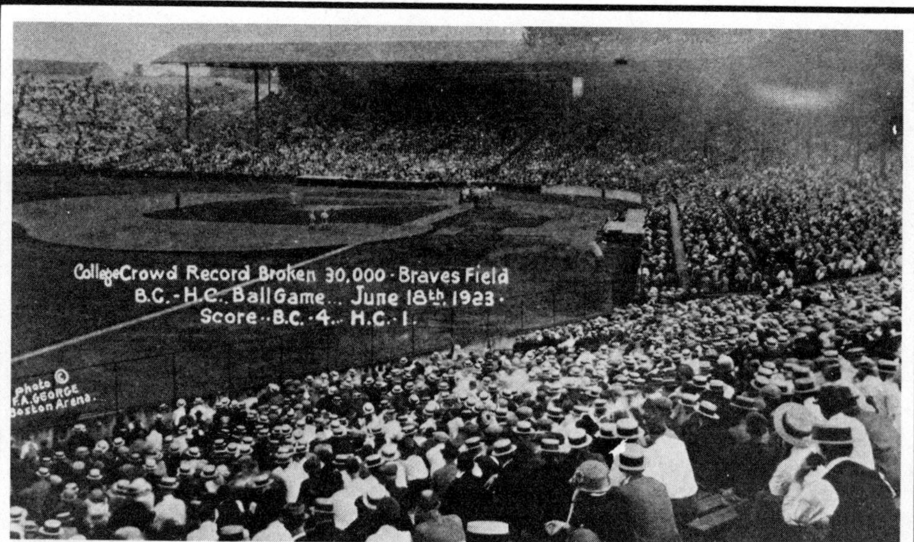

COLLEGE OF THE HOLY CROSS

Largest College Baseball Crowd

The largest crowd ever to attend an intercollegiate baseball game converged on Braves Field in Boston, Massachusetts, on June 18, 1923. The legendary game, a battle between Boston College and Holy Cross that was pivotal to the championship hopes of both, drew 35,000 spectators. Boston College won, four to one.

Longest Night of Baseball

A doubleheader played at Boston's Fenway Park between the Red Sox and the Texas Rangers during the 1977 season was the longest night in New England baseball history. The first game started at 6 PM on Wednesday, August 24, and the second game ended at 2:26 AM on Thursday, August 25. Rain was the cause of the delay.

First Night Baseball Game

New England's first night baseball game was held at Nantasket Beach, Massachusetts, in September of 1880. The field was strung with electric lights which had only been invented the year before by Thomas Alva Edison.

First All-Star Baseball Game

The Major Leagues fall fourteen years behind Massachusetts for the distinction of having the first all-star baseball game. North Attleboro and Attleboro, Massachusetts, decided in 1919 to hold a "skys-the-limit" all-star baseball game, with two teams made up of the best ball players available. Manager of the North Attleboro team, Frank Kelley, started the ball rolling when he applied to the Philadelphia Phillies' manager for a pitcher and was offered a young man by the name of Mannix. Soon both teams were applying for the loan of more professional players for their all-star game. Pro players found a gold mine in the event and didn't mind playing at all. Such baseball greats as Babe Ruth (at the height of his career) played that year along with Jim Thorpe, Hank Gowdy, and Grover Cleveland Alexander. The fans numbered 8,000 at the final game of the five-game series.

First Intercollegiate Baseball Game

Amherst College defeated Williams College (73-32) in twenty-six innings during the country's first intercollegiate baseball game in 1859.

Best Baseball Lawyer

Jerry Kapstein, acting as the legal counsel for sixty-two athletes, represents more major-league baseball players than any other attorney in New England.

Best Hockey Player

One-time Boston Bruins' hockey superstar, Bobby Orr, set numerous records during the 1969-70 hockey season, many of which may never be equaled. He won the Norris Trophy for outstanding defenseman, the Hart Trophy for the most valuable player, the Ross Trophy for NHL scoring champion, and the Conn Smythe Trophy for most valuable player in play-offs. He also scored the most points (120) in one season by an individual player, and the most points by a defenseman in Stanley Cup Play-offs.

Only Three-Team Athlete

Gene Conley was the only athlete to ever play on three big-league Boston teams: the Boston Braves, the Boston Red Sox, and the Boston Celtics.

Smallest Town with Pro Team

Foxboro, Massachusetts, is the only town of its size which can boast a national, professional sports team. Foxboro numbers only 14,000 but the population soars during football season when the fans swarm to Schaefer Stadium to watch the New England Patriots in action.

First Downhill Cyclist

James Farnsworth III of Gilmanton, New Hampshire, was the first cyclist to be clocked descending Mount Washington. Each year since 1971, on his birthday, Farnsworth cycles to the top of Mount Washington. In 1972, he cycled to the top as usual (setting a record, by the way, of one hour, forty minutes, and ten seconds) then proceeded to race down! He arrived at the bottom in nineteen minutes and fifty-five seconds.

Largest Tuna Tournament

An annual event, the Rhode Island Tuna Tournament, traditionally held over the Labor Day weekend, is the largest event of its kind in the world. And on August 21, 1977, in the preliminary rodeo for anglers to qualify for the big event, a tournament record was set. Aime Thuotte, a member of the Galilee Tuna Club, brought in a prize catch — a 1,039 pound tuna, the largest fish ever caught in Rhode Island waters by a Rhode Island fisherman.

First to Teach Basketball

While teaching at the International YMCA Training School, later to become Springfield College, in Springfield, Massachusetts, James Naismith developed a game to keep the boys fit after football season. Using a large ball, two peach baskets, and a lot of running in-between, Naismith wrote up thirteen rules to minimize physical injury while promoting the greatest amount of exercise. Springfield, the home of the first basketball game and team, is now the home of the Naismith Basketball Hall of Fame.

First Pony Races

Pony racing had its beginnings when the first New England farmers challenged their neighbors to a run for their money, but the sport has only been organized since 1946. Howard Small of Yarmouth, Maine, is widely regarded as its founder; he introduced pony racing at the state's country fairs. Small's daughter, Jane, owned a pony named "Meteor Magic" who is also a record holder: he has won more races than any horse or pony in the history of racing; 219 first places, thirty-nine second, and five third. Another distinction for Jane's horse: he ran a half mile in one minute, twenty-six seconds.

First Football Team

Organized in Boston, Massachusetts, in 1862, the Oneida Football Club was America's first football team. As a semi-professional team whose players almost all attended Mr. Dinwell's private school, the team played other schools in the area. The game, using a hard rubber ball, was played without any rest periods; each team tried to get the ball across the goal line by any means possible — and the goal line was drawn down the center of the field. The players managed to keep in touch, and surviving members of this historic team were photographed (above) when they assembled for a reunion on November 21, 1925.

First and Last Bathtub Race

When the Orleans (Massachusetts) Yacht Club's entertainment committee planned the Bathtub Race in 1976, little did they know it would be such a memorable affair, or, that this first race would also be the last they would ever plan. Twenty-eight enterprising sailors showed up at race time and the rules committee inspected each vessel to make sure it complied with the regulations. The race itself got off to a slow start; a few entries could not get past the starting line and most contestants never reached the first mile marker. After two miles, several hours, and gallons of beer, the winner, Merv Hammett, a noted Orleans sailor, crossed the finish line. Only seven vessels finished the race and about one third got nowhere and had to be towed in.

Courtesy of Florence O'Donnell

Largest Bicycle/Boat Race

Each year since its beginning in 1967, the Great Race has attracted thousands of participants, making it the largest bike and boat race in New England. The offshoot of an argument as to whether the fastest commute from Watertown to Marblehead (Massachusetts) is by land or sea, the twenty-three-mile event is open to canoes, boats, runners, and cyclists.

Oldest Foot Race

The Bemis Pie Race held at the Mount Herman School in Northfield, Massachusetts, is the oldest foot race in the United States. In 1891, six years prior to the running of the Boston Marathon, the first Bemis Pie Race took place. One hundred and forty-three men entered and ran the six-mile course along the banks of the Connecticut River. Their prize? — What else but a pie!

BOSTON MARATHON RECORDS

The Boston Marathon, first run in 1897, is New England's most famous race, and is the oldest amateur foot race in America. It is considered by most runners to also be the most grueling, and even more difficult than the Olympic Marathon. (An Olympic champ has never won the Boston Marathon.) Held annually on April 19, the Marathon now attracts several thousand runners, who test their strength against the twenty-six mile, 385-yard course from Hopkinton to Boston.

Longest Running Runner

John J. (The Elder) Kelley has run in the Boston Marathon since 1931, finishing in the first ten no less than nineteen times, winning twice, and making second place seven times! He is the most famous runner.

Hottest Marathon

Despite temperatures of ninety-one degrees in the shade and 116 on the course, the 1976 Boston Marathon was run as usual, and went on record as the hottest ever. This race was nicknamed the "Run for the Hoses" because the runners ran through innumerable sprays of water from garden hoses kindly turned on them by homeowners. Only forty percent of the 1,898 starters finished.

First Female Runner

The first woman to run in the Boston Marathon was Roberta Louise Gibb, who ran unnoticed in 1966 by officials who did not allow women to run at all. By concealing herself in a thicket until the race began, she entered and ran the entire race in roughly three-and-one-half hours. Very few people believed a woman could endure such a race and most felt she must have cheated. Women were officially admitted six years later.

Best Woman Runner

The woman's world record for marathon racing was set in 1975 in the Boston Marathon by Liane Winter. Her time was two hours, forty-two minutes, and twenty-four seconds.

Best Male Runner

In the 1975 Marathon, Will Rogers, a twenty-seven-year-old Boston College student from Connecticut, set a speed record. He finished in the record-breaking time of two hours, nine minutes, and fifty-five seconds. He stopped four times along the way for water and once to tie his shoelace.

TIM CARLSON, STOCK/BOSTON

Oldest "Flying Horse"

The oldest "flying horse" merry-go-round in America is located in Watch Hill, Rhode Island. It was brought to its present site around 1883 by an ex-circus performer named Hager. The "Flying Horse" is not a carousel per se: its horses are not attached to the floor but rather swing out in merry-go-round fashion.

Oldest Carousel

Bob and Mary Lucas own and operate America's oldest carousel, located in Oak Bluffs on Martha's Vineyard, Massachusetts. Their carousel was constructed by C. W. F. Dare Company in 1876, and was brought to Oak Bluffs from Coney Island in 1884. When it arrived it was one of the only amusements for vacationers to the island. The present owners have restored the carousel by studying paintings that showed its original decorations. The twenty hand-carved and painted horses are a beautiful example of the artistry of America's early craftsmen.

First Amusement Park

Lake Compounce Amusement Park in Bristol, Connecticut, was the first amusement park in America. Gad Norton owned a piece of lakefront property, and in 1846 came up with the idea to construct picnic tables, row boats, and bowling alleys for his friends and relatives to enjoy. He started the first partnership with his neighbor and relative Isaac Pierce in 1851. Norton's descendents still operate the park today.

First Alpine Slide

Long before the modern alpine slides that are found in New England today came to be, employees of the Mount Washington cog railroad knew the thrills of sliding down mountains on tracks. Patrick Camden, former roadmaster, is shown here, seated on a "Devil's Shingle." The piece of equipment, also known as a slideboard, was a sled of wood and metal designed to fit onto the rails, and used to transport people from the top to the bottom — in a hurry. Its speed was controlled by lifting up on the friction brake handles on either side. The record slide from the summit to the Ammonoosuc River, a distance of three miles, was two minutes and forty-five seconds. After a death, they stopped being used.

Largest Baseball Glove

Some year around 1930, a sporting goods firm in Plymouth, New Hampshire, made the largest fielders glove ever heard of in these parts. "I've seen players who needed one as big as that," said Coach Delmer Borah of the Newburyport (Massachusetts) High School Team, when a player wore the gigantic glove for practice one day. Later, E. Edward Whitley of Newburyport secured the glove for his son who loved baseball. We don't have the dimensions of the glove but it surely is the biggest we've ever seen.

Largest Bicycle

In the late 1800s, Charles Metz built a ten-seat bicycle in his Waltham, Massachusetts, bicycle factory. The twenty-two-foot, nine-inch-long bicycle is the only one of its kind in the world and has never been duplicated, probably because the cost of manufacturing one ($1200 even then) today would be prohibitive. Charles Metz's reason for building such an expensive monster was simple; he loved publicity. With ten "bloomer girls" riding the phenomenal ten-seater across America and Europe, Metz certainly won his share of publicity!

First Kiddie Kar

Clarence White of North Bennington, Vermont, constructed a straddle car for his young son, which was the first of its kind in New England. Tired of fixing broken toys which were never meant to be ridden in the first place, White decided to make a small car that his son could ride and that would stand up under the battering a little child would give. In 1915, he finished and patented the first car which he made in his father's stereoscope factory. Soon Kiddie Kars were being sold and shipped all over the United States from the modest factory in North Bennington.

Largest Gym

Located on the campus of Yale University in New Haven, Connecticut, the Payne Whitney Gymnasium is the largest gymnasium in New England, and possibly in the world. Nine-and-a-half stories tall, the complex contains two large swimming pools, twenty-eight squash courts, eight handball courts, three basketball courts, two jogging tracks, three rowing tanks, a steam room, massage room, hot room, drying room, wrestling room, weight room, fencing room, gymnastics room, dance studio, judo room, therapeutic exercise room, photography room, classrooms, and a memorial lecture room.

Largest Kite

Five young men in Terryville, Connecticut, created a sensation in 1887 when they built and successfully flew the largest kite in the United States. Launched on Thanksgiving Day, the kite was sixteen feet high, and twelve feet wide; it was covered with fifty-four feet of cloth and had a tail that measured 104 feet. After its debut, the kite's design was modified, and it was launched again.

Most Famous Kite Man

Samuel F. Perkins of Boston, Massachusetts, was the most famous kite man in New England. Visiting the Blue Hill observatory in Milton, Massachusetts, at the age of eight, he was fascinated by a reenactment of Franklin's kite experiment. Perkins became a kite man then and began to build and fly kites. He traveled throughout the country and in Europe giving kite demonstrations and participated in the famous air meet of 1910 in Quincy, Massachusetts,* flying with the greats from all over the world. Finally he made the "airplane kite," (a variation of one made by Alexander Graham Bell) which he patented in 1917.

** The great air meet of 1910 in Quincy was sponsored by the Harvard Aeronautical Society and is considered to be the first large air meet held in the western world.*

First Sneakers

America's first sports sneakers were manufactured by Marquis M. Converse of Malden, Massachusetts, in 1909. A company bearing his name is still operating, and now produces many styles of running shoes and rubber items.

Longest Ice Skates

The world's longest ice skates, twenty-four inches long, were handcrafted in New England. They combine a facility for both skiing and ice skating, a desired attribute in cross-country traveling. They are presently preserved in a private New England collection.

Fastest Ax

David Geer of Jewett City, Connecticut, without a doubt wields the fastest ax in New England. In his forty years of "professional" woodchopping, he has won five world competitions, (the first in Albany, Oregon) by out-chopping his contenders. He can cut a ten-inch-square timber block in fourteen seconds, and halve a white pine log, fourteen inches in diameter, in less than thirty and cut, split, and stack a cord of wood in forty-five minutes. Geer attests to the fact that you don't have to be a Goliath to win woodchopping competitions; he stands just five feet, seven inches tall, and weighs about 195 pounds.

First to Break Speed Record

On January 26, 1906, Fred Marriot of Watertown, Massachusetts, broke the world's speed record in a bullet-shaped Stanley Steamer. Fred got his machine going a record-breaking speed of 127.659 miles per hour at Daytona Beach, Florida. This was faster than two miles a minute. The "rocket" was steered by a tiller and weighed 1,600 pounds.

Largest Top Maker

During the great era of toy top popularity, from 1890 to 1942, the A.N. Wetherbee Mill in Lyndonville, Vermont, became the world's largest top manufacturer, shipping out as many as 5.5 million tops in a single year. The industry was closed down by the War Production Board in 1942, because the metal and lumber were needed for defense.

Only Yoyo Champion

Larry Sayco of Cumberland, Rhode Island, is the world's yoyo champion, and the only New Englander to achieve such fame. After winning a number of local competitions, Larry was offered a job by the Duncan Yoyo Company, demonstrating and promoting the toy. Sponsored by this company, Larry attended competitions, winning his first title in 1955, and his last in 1963, in Manilla.

First Yoyos

Pictured above are the first yoyos, patented in the United States in October, 1906. Llewelyn D. Lothrop and Hans Liebreich of Gloucester, Massachusetts, began making metal yoyos in the back room of Lothrop's store, located on the corner of what was then Ivy Court and Duncan Street.* As described in the patent, the toy benefits the operator "resulting from exercising of his arms and other members of the body." Though Duncan Tops Company of Lucks, Wisconsin, has patented the name "yoyo" since 1927, Lothrop and Liebreich hold the first patent for the "toy."

**Lothrop is also the inventor of the famous groaning foghorn and a brass cannon used to celebrate the Fourth of July in Gloucester.*

Only Winter Surfing Contest

Held each year in February, the only winter surfing contest in New England is the Mid-Winter Surfing Championships at the Narragansett Town Beach in Narragansett, Rhode Island.

First Women's Sport

James Plimpton made possible the first accepted women's sport when he invented the famous Plimpton roller skate in 1863. With Plimpton's skate, which could turn corners and maneuver to avoid dangerous mishaps, women could take healthful exercise out of doors which was deemed fully respectable by clergy and laymen alike. (They first practiced skating indoors, in parlors.) Up to this time women's only sport was walking or housework! Plimpton built rinks all over the nation and rented skates so that everyone could participate in the new sport, called "rinking."

First Scrabble Game

The popular game of Scrabble appeared on the American scene for the first time when it was introduced by the Production and Marketing Company of Newtown, Connecticut, in 1948.

Greatest Chess Player

Born on December 5, 1872, in Somerville, Massachusetts, Harry Nelson Pillsbury is remembered as the best chess player of them all. But Harry didn't always play an ordinary chess game. He could play blindfolded from the opposite corner of the room! That was nothing — he could simultaneously play twelve games of chess and six games of checkers plus a few rubbers of whist to ward off possible ennui. In 1895, at age twenty-two, Harry represented America at the Hastings Tournament in England. He won against Dr. Siegbert Tarrasch of Germany in one of the best chess games ever played.

Longest Balloon Flight

Ed Yost took off from the little town of Milbridge, Maine, on October 5, 1976, in an attempt to fly his helium balloon in the first manned balloon flight across the Atlantic. He didn't succeed in his endeavor, but in the process of trying he completed the longest manned balloon flight in the history of aeronautics. The "Silver Fox," as his balloon was named, remained airborne for 107 hours and thirty-seven minutes, breaking the previous record of eighty-seven hours.

First Public Playground

Up until the latter part of the nineteenth century, children in urban areas were subject to dangers of playing in the street. In 1889, an attorney named Joseph Lee improved upon the idea of the "sand garden," and despite opposition, established the first playground in America, on Boston's Columbus Avenue.

Only Three-Day Driving Event

The Myopia Three-Day Driving Event, held annually in Hamilton, Massachusetts, since 1975, is the only three-day competition in the country specifically for horses and carriages.

Largest Rocking Horse

The world's largest rocking horse stands on the grounds of the Morton E. Converse Toy Manufacturers in Winchendon, Massachusetts. Weighing a ton and a half, and standing ten feet tall, the hand-carved giant seen today (built in 1962) is an exact replica of the first such horse given to the town in 1914.

First Golf Tee

George Grant of Boston, Massachusetts, famous for his work in the treatment of cleft palate at Harvard Dental School, also invented the golf tee, in 1899. He became no richer for his discovery.

BOSTON GLOBE

Bravest Swimmers

Members of the L Street Brownies, Inc., many of whom are over seventy years of age, swim outdoors in freezing winter temperatures. The Brownies were chartered in the early 1940s and are affiliated with the L Street Bathhouse in South Boston, Massachusetts, which, incidentally, was the first free bathhouse in America. Andrew Hagerty, first president of the group and active member, tells of one member who would cut a hole in the ice to take his daily swim. To tackle winter weather with no protection but bathing suits undoubtedly make the Brownies the bravest swimmers in all of New England.

Hardiest Sailors

Every winter weekend regardless of rain, snow, sleet, etc. the Marblehead Frostbite Sailing Club meets under sail on the waters off Marblehead, Massachusetts. Undeniably this makes them the hardiest sailors in New England. In 1948, snowbound and restless men and women from various sailing groups formed the Frostbite Club for weekend sailing whatever the weather. Numbering well over 100, the club is an international class whose membership includes all ages.

Oldest Mountaineering Club

Known locally as the AMC, the Appalachian Mountain Club is the oldest moutaineering club in the western hemisphere. It was founded in February of 1876 in Boston and its first president was Professor Edward C. Pickering.

Oldest Yacht Club

The Boston Yacht Club, 111 years old, qualifies as the oldest yacht club in the country. Originally organized on September 19, 1866, its first headquarters were at 14 Tremont Street. The club moved to Marblehead via a series of mergers with other clubs, finally ending when it merged with the Marblehead Yacht Club.

First Mushroom Club

America's first mushroom club was founded in 1890 by Dr. Charles McIlvaine of Harvard University's biology department. (Dr. McIlvaine also wrote the book, *A Thousand Mushrooms.*) Today, the club's 450 mycologists come from all over the world, mostly from the United States and Mexico; they go mushroom hunting every Sunday and attend classes to learn more about the different kinds of mushrooms.

Largest Credit Card Collection

An extensive collection of credit cards, the most that we have ever seen at one time, belongs to John M. Black of Windsor, Connecticut. Representing retail stores, oil companies, airlines, banks, entertainment concerns, and novelty shops, Black's collection was started as proof that an American can gain a lot of credit with very little money.

Courtesy of Mike Sheridan

Largest Police Doll Collection

Police Chief Francis G. Reynolds of West Hartford, Connecticut, owns New England's largest collection of police dolls. Ranging in size from one inch to two feet, the statues and figurines represent all types of law enforcement officials from many different countries.

Courtesy of Mike Sheridan

Only Elephant Hair Collection

America's only elephant hair collection was compiled by Charles Davis, an elephant biographer from Hartford, Connecticut, who began his hobby in 1882. His collection consists of photographs, ivory, and more than 600 hairs from elephants' tails. (The only hairs that grow on a mature elephant's body are tail hairs and whiskers.)

Largest News Clipping Collection

The country's largest private collection of news clippings was started in the late 1930s by William R. Pratt of Lynn, Massachusetts, known to his friends as the Yankee Clipper. Tracing the historic, social, political, and economic development of America, Pratt's collection consists of more than 4 million articles from newspapers and magazines.

Courtesy of Philip Moshcovitz

Largest Dairy Collection

Russell Martin of West Greenwich, Rhode Island, has what seems to be New England's largest collection of dairy paraphernalia, consisting of over 9,000 milk bottle caps and more than 300 bottles.

Largest Auto Ad Collection

Ken Ruddock, of Stratford, Connecticut, has a collection of several thousand automobile advertisements, spanning the years from 1905 to 1970. By all our accounts, this is the largest such collection in New England.

Largest Joke Collection

Dick Cronin of Harvard, Massachusetts, maintains the largest private joke collection we know of in New England. He began collecting jokes in 1950 when he was working in public relations in Pittsfield. At last count his library contained 5,500 jokes, all organized into about eighty-five categories.

10
The Great Outdoors

First Public Land

Boston Common in Boston, Massachusetts, was established in 1634 as a "place for a trayning field" and for "the feeding of cattell." Although it was not utilized for recreation until much later, it was the first land in the country officially designated for public use.

First Publicly Funded Park

In 1853, the citizens of Hartford, Connecticut, led by Horace Bushnell, a local minister, appropriated $163,800 for the purchase of a low, swampy area of the city. Bushnell Park, designed by Frederick Law Olmstead, was the first public park in the United States to be purchased with public funds.

First Park on Donated Land

Elm Park in Worcester, Massachusetts, was established in 1854 on swamp land donated by Levi Lincoln and John Hammond. It was the first recreational park in the country to be built on land donated for public use.

Largest Fenced Park

Although it has been subdivided and broken up today, Corbin Park in Croyden, New Hampshire, was at one time the largest park in the United States entirely surrounded by a fence. It was established around 1910 as a game preserve, complete with buffalo and later wild boar, and used by notable hunters such as Teddy Roosevelt and Thomas Edison. Witnesses recall that the park continued for more than four miles on a side.

Clarence Humphrey poses at left with his 301-pound pumpkin, the largest squash ever grown in the United States.

Oldest Nudist Colony

Laurel Ridge, Inc. (Solair Recreational League) in Southbridge, Massachusetts, was established in 1940, and is the oldest and largest nudist colony in New England.

First Thornless Rose

Thornless Beauty, the world's first thornless rose, was developed after years of painstaking work by Nicholas Grillo of Milldale, Connecticut, in 1937.

Largest Rose Garden

Llys-Yr-Rhosyn in Barrington, Rhode Island, is the largest non commercial rose garden in New England. Covering eleven-and-a-half acres, the garden's name in Welsh means "Royal Court of Roses."

Only Authentic Bonsai Garden

Walt Killam's Golden Hotai Bonsai Gardens in Chester, Connecticut, is New England's only commercial bonsai producer designed as an authentic Japanese rock garden. In addition to the bonsai plants — native American plants dwarfed by ancient oriental methods utilizing weights, clamps, and wires — the garden contains a gourd-shaped pool, a waterfall, a Zen section, and a five-foot gilded statue of Hotai.

Largest Arboretum

With its main portion covering 265 acres of Jamaica Plain, Massachusetts, Arnold Arboretum is the largest such park in New England. Case Estates, also officially part of the arboretum although not generally included in discussions, covers an additional 165 acres in the nearby town of Weston.

CHAMPION TREES

Largest Pitch Pine

Ninety-six feet tall, with a circumference of eleven feet and four inches, and an average crown spread of fifty feet, the largest pitch pine in the country stands near Thompson Lake in Poland, Maine.

Largest Pussy Willow

The largest pussy willow in America is located in Wilmington, Massachusetts. It is forty feet tall, has a circumference of five feet and two inches, and spreads forty-five feet across at the crown.

Largest Sweet Birch

Standing near New Boston, New Hampshire, the country's largest sweet birch tree is seventy feet high, has a circumference of fifteen feet and two inches, and an average crown spread of eighty-seven feet.

Largest Tamarack

Located in a swamp in Jay, Maine, the country's largest tamarack is ninety-five feet high, has a circumference of thirty-seven inches, and an average crown spread of fifty feet.

Largest White Birch

The largest white birch in the country is ninety-six feet high, eighteen feet and one inch around, and has a crown spread of eighty-three feet. It stands off a logging road in Hartford, Maine.

Largest White Pine

Standing near Blanchard, Maine, the largest white pine in the United States is 147 feet tall, and has a circumference of eighteen feet and two inches with an average crown spread of just over seventy-three feet.

Largest Spruce

The largest spruce tree in America stands 108 feet from roots to tip. Located near Durham, New Hampshire, the huge tree has a circumference of fifteen feet and six inches. Its crown spread averages out to be fifty-five feet.

Courtesy of American Forestry Association

PRESERVATION SOCIETY OF NEWPORT COUNTY

Only Animal Garden

Started by Thomas Brayton around 1880, Green Animals in Portsmouth, Rhode Island, is New England's only garden to feature large bushes, shrubs, and trees sculpted into the shape of animals.

First Lilac Tree

Still growing beside the Governor Benning Wentworth House at Little Harbor in Portsmouth, New Hampshire, the first lilac bush ever planted in the United States was set into the ground by the settlers of Strawbery Banke in 1750.

Oldest Linden Tree

A very large linden tree, more than fifteen feet in circumference, grows in the front yard of the Wentworth-Gardner House in Portsmouth, New Hampshire. Planted by Thomas Wentworth in 1760, it is the oldest such tree in the United States.

Only State Pine

Vermont's state seal features a pine tree which still stands, over 300 years old now, on town-owned land off Route 313 in Arlington, Vermont. Although time and several bills before Congress have changed the face slightly from its original design of 1779, the State Pine is still prominent on the seal.

Only Kin of Newton's Apple Tree

Ensconced in the campus of Babson College in Wellesley, Massachusetts, since 1954, New England's only living descendent of Sir Isaac Newton's famous apple tree continues to drop apples and inspire great minds.

AUBREY P. JANION

Last Connecticut Log Drive

The last log drive ever held on the Connecticut River, in the spring and summer of 1909, was also the largest in the history of the river. The drive, which began April 6, contained 40 million feet of lumber, and employed a rear crew of sixty men. This was also the last log drive for the leader, Henry Van Dyke, whose chauffeur drove the car off a cliff as they sat watching the drive's progress.

Northernmost White Cedar Stand

A group of Atlantic white cedar trees in the midst of the Bradford Bog in Bradford, New Hampshire, is farther north than any other group of the same species in the United States. The area is managed by the New England Wild Flower Society.

Largest Alpine Zone

New England contains the largest alpine zone east of the Mississippi River, the Alpine Garden, located on Mt. Washington between Lion's Head and Nelson Craig in the midst of New Hampshire's White Mountain National Forest. In addition to sixty-four species of alpine shrubs, plants, mosses, and alpine flowers, three species of insects are found here which exist nowhere else in New England — *Brenthis montinus* and *Oeneis melissa semidea,* butterflies, and *Autographa interrogationis uruareum,* a moth.

Only Northward River

Running through southwestern New Hampshire, the Contoocook River is the only continuously north flowing river in New England.

Most Water Area

New Hampshire has more water area than any other state in the country in proportion to its size.

Only Magnetic Hill

Lowe Street in Leominster, Massachusetts, is the only hill in New England reputed to have the "magnetic" power to pull an unmanned automobile uphill. Sophisticated measurements, however, have revealed that despite its completely flat appearance the disputed portion of Lowe Street has an imperceptible downhill grade and it is simple gravity that makes the cars roll.

Most Monadnocks

New Hampshire has five mountains that all bear the name Monadnock, a distinction, albeit a confusing one, for the Granite State.

Oldest Limestone Quarry

History has recorded that a quarry called Limerock in Lincoln, Rhode Island, was opened in 1643 by Thomas Harris, making it the oldest limestone quarry in the United States.

Deepest Limestone Quarry

Although it is now filled with water, the limestone quarry in Rockland, Maine, is the deepest such quarry in the world, extending down to 400 feet.

Northernmost Anthracite Bed

The bed of anthracite coal found in the islands of Narragansett Bay, Rhode Island, holds a record for lying farther north than any other such bed in the country.

Most Dangerous Gorge

Known locally as Killer Gorge, the ravine cut by the Huntington River through Richmond, Vermont, is the most dangerous river gorge in New England. The official death count has reached eleven since 1950, but old-timers around town would put it closer to thirty. Filled with strong currents, whirlpools, and underwater ledges that trap even the ablest swimmers, the gorge remains a favorite "swimming hole" for young thrill seekers. Although there was a considerable amount of publicity about the treacherous pass after a particularly gruesome double drowning in 1969, and rumors circulated about both the state and the federal government attempting to purchase the land to make it into a patrolled state park, nothing has been done yet. The owner did dynamite one of the most culpable underwater ledges in 1973; but five young swimmers have drowned since then.

Largest Serpentine Rock

A thirty to forty-ton rock, deposited by a glacier in Grafton, Vermont, is the largest mass of serpentine in North America.

Largest Granite Quarry

Barre, Vermont, is the home of the largest granite quarry in the world, The Rock of Ages Quarry, which covers twenty-four acres and extends to a depth of 265 feet.

Oldest Inscribed Rock

Dighton Rock, now enclosed in a pavilion in Berkley, Massachusetts, is the oldest inscribed rock in North America. The dominant theory, that the rock was marked by early Portuguese explorers, was initiated in 1918 when Professor Edmund Delabarre of Brown University discovered that the date 1511, the name of the Portuguese navigator Miguel Corte Real, and the Portuguese coat-of-arms were inscribed in the rock.

Maine's Largest Rock

Daggett's Rock, on Griscom's farm in Phillips, Maine, is the largest rock in that state. The above-ground portion of the boulder measures thirty-one feet high, 100 feet long, and fifty-five feet wide; its weight is approximately 8,000 tons.

New Hampshire's Largest Rock

Rumored to have once been the top of nearby Mt. Chocorua, the Madison Boulder in Madison, New Hampshire, is the largest in the state, measuring ninety feet long, thirty-eight feet high, and forty feet wide.

Connecticut's Largest Rock

Cochegan Rock in Montville, Connecticut, is the largest rock in the state, and has been claimed to be the largest in the country. It stands over forty-five feet high, is over fifty-eight feet long, with its total (above and below-ground) weight estimated at 10,000 tons.

Most Famous Glacial Rock

The last rock to be carried by glacier from Mt. Monadnock, New Hampshire, to the summit of Rollstone Hill, the Rollstone Boulder is the most famous glacial rock in New England. Having served as an important landmark for early settlers, the rock was moved by the Fitchburg Historical Society to its present location on Main Street in Fitchburg, Massachusetts.

Most Religious Rock

As the story goes, the inscription of the Lord's Prayer on a rock just outside of Bristol, Vermont, was carved in 1891 as a hint to profane teamsters urging their horses up a nearby hill.

Largest Balanced Rock

Deposited by a glacier north of Pontoosuc Lake near Lanesborough, Massachusetts, a 365-ton mass of limestone poised on a three-foot base of bedrock outcropping is the largest balanced rock in New England.

Only Fish Rock

The only completely natural rock that we know of in New England to be shaped remarkably like a huge fish is located in Shelburne, New Hampshire.

Only Elephant Rock

At the apex of Pike Hill, near Newport, New Hampshire, stands the only rock in New England to closely resemble an elephant at rest. The illusion is said to be especially striking when the rock is wet.

Only Forlorn Lover's Rock

When Susan Baker, who had spurned Captain John Brown continuously over the years, died unmarried at the age of 81, her forsaken lover carved the following epitaph to her on a rock: " . . . April the 9th, 1878. May God Bless Susan and all of her barren land and when she gits to heaven I hope she find a man." Brown's Boulder sits just north of Lanesborough, Massachusetts.

Most Famous Rock

Undisputedly, New England's most famous rock is Plymouth Rock, which marks the spot in Plymouth, Massachusetts, where the Pilgrims landed from the *Mayflower* on December 21, 1620.

Only Hieroglyphic Rock

Located on the west bank of the Connecticut River at Bellows Falls, Vermont, a large boulder covered with markings which have been positively identified as ancient Indian hieroglyphics is the only one of its kind in New England.

DICK SMITH

Most Famous Rock Faces

The most famous and most visible of the large stone faces engraved by nature into New England's mountain cliffs is undoubtedly the Old Man of the Mountain in Franconia, New Hampshire. But, there are several other notable "faces" such as Joshua's Mountain in Assonet, Massachusetts. Just for the record, a quarry in Graniteville, Rhode Island, also claims its own "old man."

Worst Animal Disaster

In 1872, an epidemic of horse distemper ravaged many parts of New England and had a terrific impact on business and transportation at the time. Many horses, especially in cities, were either killed or left too weak to work, and oxen and strong men took their places until the epidemic ended.

First Poultry Show

Held every year since 1849 in the Boston, Massachusetts, area, the Boston Poultry Show was the first, and is now the oldest, animal show in the country to feature exclusively poultry.

Only Native American Cat

Maine coon cats are the only native American breed of cat. All other felines are immigrants in one way or another.

Last Oxen on Martha's Vineyard

Once the main source of transportation and farming power on the island, the last oxen on Martha's Vineyard disappeared in 1864. Named Kickapoo and Jackapoo, they belonged to Jack Belain.

Largest Lobster

A prime specimen of the heaviest species of crustacean, the world's largest lobster, on display in the Museum of Science in Boston, Massachusetts, measures three feet from tail to claw and weighed forty-two pounds, seven ounces when alive. There are undocumented reports of heavier lobsters, but the Boston lobster remains the largest on record.

Largest Fresh-Water Fish

Now protected by government regulations as an endangered species, sturgeon is New England's largest fresh-water fish, and the only place the species can be found in the region is in Vermont's Lake Champlain. Although local rumors speak of 200-pound fish, the record catch was approximately seven feet long and 140 pounds. In 1964, it was rescued from an infestation of lamprey eels by Mr. and Mrs. Dudley Trombley and Dr. and Mrs. Steve Olin and later released.

Only Dog with a Hundred Owners

Chick the Wonder Coon Dog was, to the best of our knowledge, the only dog in this country to have 100 owners. Needing a good coon dog, Arthur and Ben Clark of Windsor, Connecticut, purchased Chick from a southern farmer for fifty dollars in 1937. Now that was a lot of money to spend for a dog back then, even one with a reputation as solid as Chick's, and to make up the money, the Clarks began to offer shares in the Wonder Coon Dog Corporation of America to help pay for Chick. One hundred investors from the Old Newgate Coon Club contributed a total of $425; the Clarks were then obligated by Connecticut law to have each owner's name engraved on Chick's collar. (We don't know what they did with the profit they made!) The collar was in fact printed with every name, and, a record holder without the dog, it is on display at the coon club in Norfolk.

Most Beached Blackfish

Around the turn of the century and even earlier, large schools of blackfish would occasionally become stranded on the beach in Provincetown, Massachusetts. We don't have the date or the exact number of fish for this photograph, but we're quite sure that it represents a record beaching.

Only Polar Bear Window

A polar bear window at the Worcester Science Center in Worcester, Massachusetts, is the only window in New England that permits visitors to view polar bears in their underwater environment. Installed in 1972, the four-by-eight-foot underwater structure was the first of its type in the world.

S.R. GILCREAST, JR.

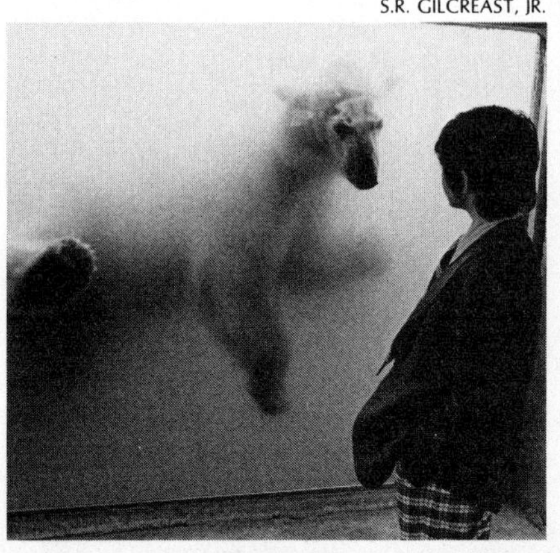

Last Cougar Shot in Vermont

Standing seven feet long and weighing 182½ pounds, the last cougar shot in Vermont was known as the Barnard Panther, killed by Alexander Crowell near Barnard in 1881. The cougar's body is stuffed and on display in the State Historical Museum adjacent to the State House in Montpelier, Vermont.

Last Fire Dog in New Haven

When the last of his cohorts died as a result of the Factory Street fire in the mid 1950s, Butch of the Savin Rock Fire Department became the last official fire dog in the New Haven, Connecticut, area. Rather high strung and prone to bark often and loudly, dalmations have been gradually taken out of service in fire departments all over New England since the advent of the two-way radio.

First Retired Horse Farm

Red Acre Farm in Stow, Massachusetts, established in 1906 by Harriet Bird, was New England's first farm and rest home for retired horses.

WILLIAM H. SANDERS

Slowest Horse

In 1910, Farmer Wilmont's steed, Slowpoke, won the twenty-five dollar purse at the Brattleboro(Vermont) Fair for taking the longest amount of time to trot the half-mile track. This makes him the slowest horse we've ever heard of; the race provides the only documented evidence of any horse's lack of speed.

Oldest Owl

Donated to the Museum of Science in Boston, Massachusetts, when he was a day-old foundling, Spooky is now the oldest owl living in captivity. He celebrated his twenty-sixth birthday on March 21, 1977.

Largest Pumpkin

Weighing in at 301 pounds with a circumference of ninety-eight inches, the largest pumpkin in the United States was grown by Clarence Humphrey in his back yard in Woburn, Massachusetts, in 1975. The secret was in the genetics: it was a cross between a Big Mack pumpkin and a Hungarian squash.

Largest Mushroom

Anthony DiBella of Weymouth, Massachusetts, discovered the largest mushroom ever found in New England, and possibly in the world. In 1972, he came upon the sixty-pound record holder growing wild in nearby Braintree, and after showing it to a number of people, he chopped it up and obtained enough pieces to fill fifteen quarts. He has since found two more giants, weighing thirty pounds and forty pounds.

Courtesy of Florence O'Donnell

Most Civic-Minded Eel

The only record of an eel being used to perform a civic duty is held by the Durham Aqueduct Company of Durham, Connecticut. At some point after the opening of the company's first public water system in 1798, the pipes became almost totally clogged with accumulated silt. To remedy the situation, local farmers procured a good-sized eel and inserted him, tail end first, into the water system's pipe at its source. The plug at the far end of the system was then removed and, try as he might to swim upstream, the eel was washed backward all the way down the pipe, pushing the sediment behind him. (The eel survived, and ended his six-hour journey when he landed in a brook in the center of town.)

NEW ENGLAND MERCHANTS BANK

First Concord Grape

As a result of meticulous cross-breeding, Ephraim Bull developed the Concord grape in Concord, Massachusetts. Planted in 1843, the vines produced their first fruit in 1849, were first exhibited in 1853 at the Massachusetts Horticultural Society in Boston, and were first marketed by Hovey and Company of Boston in 1854. By 1855, the famous grapes were being grown throughout the United States.

Largest Egg

In 1974, the world's largest egg was shown at the Central Maine Egg Festival. Laid by a hen belonging to Richard Jose of Stockton, Maine, the prize ovum displaced 170 milliliters of water.

Largest Potato Harvest

The year 1816 brought some peculiar and profound weather to New England including unusual conditions for the greatest potato harvest we've ever heard of. Jacob Carr of Weare, New Hampshire, boasted of potatoes he picked that year that ran 500 bushels to an acre and nary a one was picked up until it was the size of a tea kettle.

Finest Asparagus

For many years, Hadley, Massachusetts, "The Asparagus Capital of the World," has produced the sweetest and crispest asparagus in the country. As asparagus is a delicate crop, it must be picked early in the morning before it wilts in the noonday heat. In Hadley's ideal growing conditions, a single spear will grow to its full height of seven inches in a single day. And as far as we're concerned, the Rytuba family in Hadley who planted their first "grass" in 1927, grows the finest crop there is.

Best Sauerkraut

Morse's farm in Waldoboro, Maine, is the home of the world's best sauerkraut. Produced from September through February, none of the sixty-five or seventy tons of kraut and juice are canned or frozen; it is all sold fresh to customers who come up the driveway. And that's the way it has been since 1910, when the family business started.

First Four-Leaf Clover Grower

When Archer F. Herrick of Saco, Maine, discovered a four-leaf clover in his backyard, he proceeded to become the first New Englander to cultivate an entire line of multi-leafed clover plants. By the mid 1940s, having perfected a plant which produced only four-leaf clovers, Herrick sold some of his specimens and sent many to "the boys overseas."

GREAT DEBATE

Where Does the Sun Rise First?

Of course the sun rises first on West Quoddy Head, the easternmost point on the Maine coast. Or does it rise first on Mt. Katahdin, 140 miles northwest of West Quoddy Head but with an elevation 5,268 feet higher? Or perhaps on Mars Hill, bordering New Brunswick, Canada, with an elevation of 1,660 feet? Or even Cadillac Mountain, on the coast at Bar Harbor?

The argument over where in the United States the sun rises first has been disputed by down-easters for years, and it is only with some fairly complex scientific calculations of the angle of the sun, the date, and the specific elevations that conclusions can finally be drawn. After considerable consternation and fancy figuring, we have come up with the following answer, but you must remember that the dates are all approximate, and all of these sunrises occur within minutes of each other.

From December 21 to March 6, the sun shines first on Cadillac Mountain; from March 7 to March 24 on West Quoddy Head; from March 25 to September 18 on Mars Hill; from September 19 to October 6 on West Quoddy Head again; and from October 7 to December 20 on Cadillac Mountain. The only notable exceptions to this rule occur when New Brunswick hills occasionally obscure the West Quoddy Head view, giving the distinction back to Cadillac Mountain, or the Mars Hill view, giving Mt. Katahdin the sun's first rays.

Courtesy of Blanton C. Wiggin

Most Knowledgeable Bean Man

John Withee of Lynnfield, Massachusetts, is the undisputed New England authority on bean raising and cooking. Mr. Withee, a retired medical photographer, has dedicated his life to the preservation of America's heirloom beans, those older species in danger of dying out. Although he has less than an acre of land himself, he manages to perpetuate upwards of 300 varieties of beans.

First Practical Snow Management

Used simply to pack down the deep New England snows on well-traveled thoroughfares, snow rollers, such as the one pictured here, were the first practical method of managing snow. Replacing the much less effective custom of dragging a heavy log behind a horse-drawn sled, snow rollers were pulled by horses or oxen and enjoyed tremendous popularity during the late 1800s and early 1900s, but were almost all replaced with more modern snowplows by 1935.

Coldest Summer

The summer of 1816 was the coldest summer that New England has ever seen. According to accounts from the time, several people froze to death in the great snowstorm of June 17. Most of the New England corn crop failed; one farmer in Tewksbury, Vermont, built fires around his cornfield every night to keep off the frost, which enabled him to harvest the only crop in the region that year. Huge hailstones beat the blossoms off all the fruit trees, and so many birds froze to death that the bird population didn't resume normal proportions for several years afterward. Sheep, cattle, and pigs froze to death in their enclosures, leading to near famine on many farms. A lake in Massachusetts was frozen solid enough to support the weight of a man, and a well in Lyman, New Hampshire, remained firmly frozen eight feet below the surface of the earth from July 4 to July 25. Heavy frosts and ice storms were frequent.

Such weather had a profound effect on the mood of the people: speculations that the sun was never going to return were common, and the drought, financial panic, and lack of food were more than some could handle. Suicides were not unusual: one man became so hopeless that he killed all his cattle before he hanged himself.

No one, of course, completely understood the cause of such extreme weather conditions. Scholars blamed it on the prevalence of sunspots and the total solar eclipse of that year, but the most likely cause of such cold was a blanket of ash which, having exploded into the atmosphere during the eruption of an East Indian volcano the year before, now covered the earth like a great cosmic umbrella and effectively blocked many of the sun's summer rays.

11
Architectural Oddities

Oldest Library Building

Sturgis Library in Barnstable, Massachusetts, is the oldest building to house a library in New England.* Built in 1644 by Reverend John Lothrop, the house did not become a library until October, 1863. Sturgis, a commercial clipper ship owner, lived with his family for most of his life. With a keen interest in ideas and books, he had long wanted his home to have a library. Hence his legacy became effective after his death. After renovation of the building to accommodate the 1,300 volumes, the Sturgis Library opened its door to the public on August 2, 1867.

Oldest Library in Continuous Use

Redwood Library and Athenaeum at 50 Bellevue Avenue in Newport, Rhode Island, is the oldest library structure still dedicated to its original purpose. Incorporated in 1747, the library was started as a company under the patronage of Abraham Redwood.

First Privately Supported Library

The books in Durham, Connecticut, and the Book Company which owned them, made up the first public library collection in New England supported by private taxes and gifts. Although founded October 30, 1733, the library was changed in the 1850 s and reinstated as the Durham Public Library in 1893.

**The Sturgis Library holds another record in that it is the oldest structure standing where religious services were regularly held.*

New England's biggest architectural letdown occurred when authorities announced that Newport's tower, at left, was not built by Vikings.

First Free Public Library

America's first free public library supported by voluntary contributions opened in 1822 in Dublin, New Hampshire.

First Tax-Supported Library

In 1827, Dr. Abiel Abbot, a new minister in Peterborough, New Hampshire, organized the Peterborough Library Company, the first tax-supported free public library, incorporated in January of 1833. As a result of the town meeting on April 9, 1833, a proposal was made to give a portion of the State Literary Fund to the purchase of books as the nucleus of a library that would be owned by the people and free to all in the town.

Vermont's Oldest Meetinghouse

The First Congregational Church in Thetford, Vermont, was built in 1787 to serve both religious and political roles in the town. It is the oldest meetinghouse in continuous use in Vermont.

Only Church with Backward Pews

Built in 1830, the First Congregational Church in North Scituate, Rhode Island, has a unique seating arrangement: the pews all face the front doors, and look away from the minister! Built at a time when Indian raids were still a cause for concern, the arrangement of the pews were "at alert" for the congregation. Facing the doors, they were never in danger of a "surprise" attack, which happily, no one recalls ever happened. The choir sat at the back of the congregation and only the minister and the organist turned their backs to the doors. Although abandoned as a church more than eight years ago, the pews still face the silent doorways.

Most Records for One Church

Trinity Church in Newport, Rhode Island, was built between 1725 and 1726, and features more superlatives than any other church in New England.

Trinity features America's only three-tiered wine glass pulpit located in its original position in the center of the aisle. It is a reminder that in Puritan New England, the preaching of the Gospel was the central feature of worship. The massive sounding board over the pulpit and the iron work holding it are magnificent examples of colonial craftsmanship. One rector, uneasy with the idea of a heavy weight hanging over his head, had the sounding board removed, but, finding that his uneasiness still remained, he later allowed it to be put back in place.

Both the interior and the steeple at Trinity are thought by authorities in the field to more closely resemble Sir Christopher Wren's London churches than any other building of the period in New England.

The church contains the Kay legacy baptismal basin, built in 1734 by Newport silversmith Daniel Russell, and considered to be the greatest piece of American silver in the country. Among other famous Americans, Oliver Hazard Perry and his brother, Mathew, were baptized together in the basin in 1795.

Trinity still owns approximately forty books, remnants from an original collection of more than seventy, that formed New England's first public circulating library in the early 1700s.

In 1967, Trinity Church was chosen to become the first building in America to appear on a Wedgewood medallion. The work of art that followed the decision was designed by William B. Hoyt, a Newport artist.

Trinity's Queen Anne bell, built in 1702, was most likely the first church bell ever to ring, and consequently be heard, in New England.

When three earlier Anglican parishes in New England went out of existence, the parish at Trinity, established in 1698, became the oldest in the region.

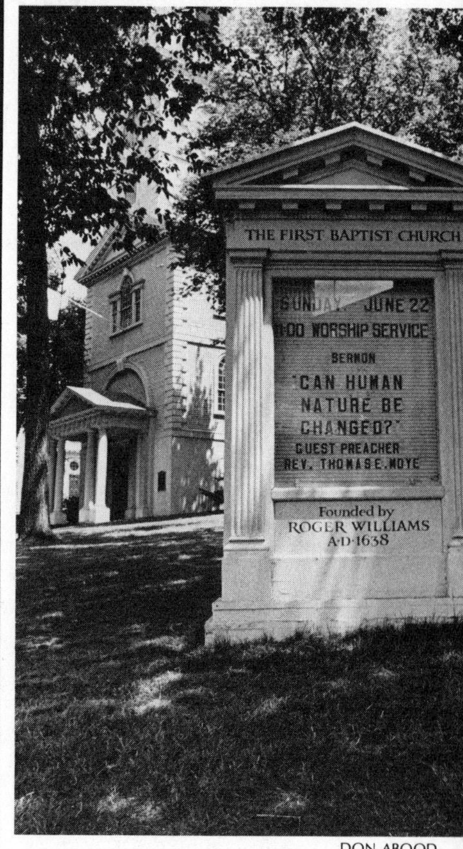

DON ABOOD

Oldest Baptist Church

Roger Williams founded America's first Baptist congregation in 1638 in Providence, Rhode Island. As the fervent group increased in membership during its early years, it met in several different buildings. The present Baptist meetinghouse in Providence, the oldest in New England, was built in 1774-1775, and is also one of the largest colonial buildings in the region.

Oldest Synagogue

Touro Synagogue in Newport, Rhode Island, is the oldest synagogue in America. Ground was broken in 1759; slowly, the work progressed beset, like most church construction, by delay and lack of funds. Finally, four years after the laying of the cornerstone, the synagogue was ready for dedication on December 2, 1763.

Only Pineapple Steeple

In 1860, an unknown person caused a pineapple, ancient symbol of hospitality, to be placed atop the North Thetford, Vermont, church spire. This steeple pineapple, the only one in such a setting in the nation, was thirty-two inches in height with an "old pine" core of sixteen inches in diameter. This wooden core was a cylinder tapering off at the top in a graceful cone. It was cut down to the pineapple shape by a lathe and through the center a hole was bored for the rod which held the complete pineapple in place on top of the church spire. In the autumn of 1957, the original was replaced with a replica; the replica now sits on the spire.

Only Medieval Wooden Church

The Old Ship Church in Hingham, Massachusetts, is the only example of medieval wooden craftsmanship on this continent.* By 1681, Hingham was a flourishing settlement of 300 people. After nearly fifty years of struggling with timber and soil, the settlers turned their energies to building a fine church. A committee was chosen to inspect churches in Cambridge and nearby towns but, spurning other examples they were shown, they decided to build the finest church on the new continent. Since the only ecclesiastical architecture they knew was that of the great Gothic churches in the Old World, the church they built was pure medieval in wood. That it is the only example of its kind on this continent lies in an event which occurred three thousand miles away in the homeland. In 1660, the Great Fire of London laid waste to vast areas of the city and destroyed 120 churches. Out of the fire of London, in the rebuilding, was born a new treatment of wood: the delicate, formalized, slender-spired churches of Sir Christopher Wren, replacing the heavier medieval style.

First YMCA

New England's first YMCA was founded in Boston in 1851 by T.V. Sullivan, a Baptist sea captain.

**The Old Ship Church also holds the record as being the oldest church in continuous service in the US.*

STEPHEN T. WHITNEY

Only Church with Hand on Top

The Methodist Church in Milton Mills, New Hampshire, dates back to the 1870s and we are reasonably sure it is the only church in the world with a pointing hand on its spire. Aratus B. Shaw, one of the villagers most inspired and most influential in establishing the church, directed the building. By the end of the summer, when enthusiasm for the project began to wane, the crew of laborers decided to cease work until spring. All agreed except Aratus. He was determined to finish the church. Alone he labored through the fall and winter, building and installing the pews. By January of 1872, he was able to turn his energy toward the adornment for the steeple. He selected a symbol that would indicate from whom he had drawn the courage and strength to see the project through — a closed fist with a forefinger pointing toward heaven. Carved from a solid block of wood, the hand is in appropriate scale for the steeple's finial. The wrist measures twenty inches in girth, the knuckles are thirty-four inches, the thumb is eight inches, and the pointing finger is eleven inches.

Only Movable Chapel

If you had been among the folk on hand in Jamestown, Rhode Island, on April 18, 1899, you'd have been treated to a sight almost as rare as a cream-colored coon cat — for that day a fully equipped church rolled down Narragansett Avenue, past the old Bay Voyage Hotel and out of town. The "Movable Chapel of the Transfiguration" gained international fame at the time of its "launching," both for itself and for the island of Conanicut (Jamestown). It commanded stories as far fielded as Cairo, Egypt, only partly because of its uniqueness. The other reason was the fire, persistence, and "ballyhoo-ability" of its inventor, the Reverend Charles E. Preston.

When he was rector at Jamestown's St. Matthew's Church, Preston got his chance to put God, progress, and a bit of America in a little package . . . up on wheels. The way his plan developed, the chapel would be moved twice a year. For ten months it would serve as a community church for the farm families about three miles north of the town. For the summer season, twenty oxen would tow the chapel two miles farther to the northern tip of the island.

Construction proceeded rapidly in

the shadow of the St. Matthew's steeple. The Archibald Wheel Works, in Lawrence, Massachusetts, manufactured the four massive wheels (two-and-a-half foot diameter in front, three-and-a-half foot in rear, with three-inch spokes). The chapel measured eighteen feet wide and twenty-seven feet long. At the rear was a small bay window, just two feet deep, to make room for the altar. The wheels, when rolling, would leave tracks over nine feet apart. A good-sized belfry, sporting a 375-pound bell presented by the Cincinnati Bell Foundry Company, was mounted jutting from the front of the building so as not to rise too high above the ridgepole. Thus the whole affair could be rolled right under strung telegraph wires. The belfry was fitted with a removable cross as well.

By April, the roads evened out in the thaw, and on the 17th, Preston conducted a short ceremony at his church on wheels. The following day the whole town and the crowds of curiosity seekers gathered for the "launching." Needless to say the movable chapel never did get to its summer quarters in Conanicut Park. After an exhausting two days with uncalculated mishaps, the Movable Chapel of the Transfiguration was moved into a plot at the top of the hill, three miles from Jamestown. Thomas G. Carr, who owned the land, offered it immediately as a permanent resting place. The following Sunday, the Reverend Preston conducted his opening services before a crowd.

The Chapel of the Transfiguration housed its last congregation in 1935, after which the diocese sold it to a family for a private home.

Courtesy of Ira Dember

Oldest Jail

The Old Gaol in York, Maine, is America's oldest extant jail. As a mute threat against the Royalists and to meet the need of a place to confine prisoners in the Province of Maine, a jail was ordered in York as early as 1653. What with inadequacies of the building, the erection of a stone cell was ordered in 1719. Necessary accommodations were added from time to time until 1806, when the building was completed as it appears today. The York Gaol confined prisoners until 1860.

DOUGLAS ARMSDEN

Oldest Blockhouse

Fort Halifax in Winslow, Maine, pictured here, is the oldest blockhouse in the United States. Part of a larger fortification, it was used as a way station for Colonel Benedict Arnold's expedition through the Maine wilderness to Quebec in 1775. The original timbers of the structure date back to 1754 and ax-chopped depressions on the exterior indicate spots where bullets were freed from the walls. This is the only remaining Maine fort constructed prior to the Revolutionary War.

S.R. GILCREAST, JR.

Oldest Tavern

Nearly 300 years old, the White Horse Tavern in Newport, Rhode Island, is the country's oldest operating tavern. It was built by William Mayes before 1673. Mayes received his liquor license in 1687 and the tavern has remained in business ever since. The building was used as a meeting place for the town council and British troops occupied it several times from 1777 to 1779.

Longest Tavern

For more than a century the old Eli Warren Tavern stood in the little village of West Upton, Massachusetts. Today it is appreciated as the longest tavern ever built in New England. Extending nearly 100 feet along its main side, this remarkable old hostelry jutted another fifty feet at right angles, as if by afterthought of its builder. Diners and roomers entered by seven separate entrances. As early as 1833, under the sponsorship of Major Warren, the rude ballroom became a mecca for dancing and "sociables."

That anything tangible remains of the Warren Tavern is due to a superstition of its one-time owner about razing a building completely. When he sent out crews to dismantle the ancient inn in 1883, the men were ordered to divide the rangy tavern into sections and distribute them as dwelling houses. Four large rooms were fashioned from the wrecked tavern. These were trundled to Mosquito Hollow, where they still stand and serve as family homes.

Courtesy of Chester W. Walker

Largest Wooden Building

The Old Griswold Hotel, which once stood on the east side of the Thames River in Groton, Connecticut, was the largest wooden building ever constructed in New England. Morton F. Plant, builder of the Griswold in 1906, would never have envisioned that his pride and joy would one day be demolished. In fact, business was so good that Plant enlarged the original two-story building by adding two more stories shortly before he died in 1918. In the '20s and '30s, the Griswold played host to the rich and the very rich. The very rich tied their yachts up at the dock and threw parties on the lawn. And in the spring when Yale and Harvard rowing teams met in desperate struggle on the Thames, the Griswold sold out every room. The hotel's eighteen-hole, 129-acre golf course supplied jobs to several generations of kids whose tips for caddying came to more in a day than they could earn in weeks doing anything else.

After the 1929 stock market crash, there weren't too many of the very rich to come to the Griswold, and the management began to book conventions and wedding parties. It was still a great hotel. During the hurricane of 1938, the dangers of a wooden structure became too apparent to Groton police and fire officials. The structure was without electricity, and it took little imagination to picture a candle in any of the 300 rooms coming in contact with lush draperies to start a disastrous fire. Fortunately no accident occurred, but it was a night remembered.

In 1959, the Griswold was purchased by Milton O. Slosberg, who modernized it. He replaced the winding paths of the rose garden with a new swimming pool, and exchanged the velvet drapes for safer, fiberglass types. A colorful folder described its charms and called it: "The Pride and Joy of All New England." Among other blandishments the hotel offered: over five miles of carpeting; new sofas and chairs for continuous seating the length of the Holland tunnel; enough mirrors to permit 1,560 women to powder their noses at the same time; and so many new bedspreads that if stitched together they would cover the Yankee Stadium.

In 1962, Slosberg Griswold Enterprises contracted to sell the Griswold Hotel to Resort Hotel, Inc. but the latter firm went bankrupt before the schedule of payments had been completed. In June of 1968, a three-day auction was held and the Griswold's furnishings were sold at unusually high prices; then in October, Charles Pfizer and Company, a major pharmaceutical concern, paid $395,000 for the old Griswold. They had the building destroyed and in that process there was no doubt that it was the largest wooden structure in New England.

Courtesy of Richard R. Towne

Largest Marble Dome

Rhode Island's capitol building in Providence features a marble dome that is the largest such unsupported structure in the United States, second only to St. Peter's in Rome. Approximately 327,000 cubic feet of white Georgia marble, 1,309 tons of iron floor beams and 15 million bricks were used in construction of the capitol. Standing atop the dome, 235 feet above the terrace and 313 feet above the mean high water mark, is the statue of the Independent Man.

First "First-Class" Hotel

In October of 1827, the Tremont House in Boston opened to the public and was known as America's first "first class" hotel. Peter C. Boone and David Sears each gave $10,000 to have it built.

Most Literary House

The House of Seven Gables, located at 54 Turner Street in Salem, Massachusetts, is outstanding for its unusual architecture, but it is perhaps even more of a record holder for its fame as the reported setting for Hawthorne's classic story. Built about 1668, the house has been carefully preserved, and is the most popular of Salem's historic sites.

Oldest Brick House

The Cradock House on Riverside Avenue in East Medford, Massachusetts, is reputedly the oldest brick house in New England. There is every reason to believe that it was built early in the spring of 1634. Unlike many early settlement homes, this house was built by the owner but intended to be run by the caretaker.

Only Hotel with a Zoo

Casco Castle in South Freeport, Maine, built by Amos F. Gerald in 1903, was the only hotel we've ever heard of that contained a zoo. Not much is known of the small collection of animals kept as one of the establishment's attractions. The hotel, offering accommodations for 100, was joined by a bridge to the stone tower which still stands. Contrary to some reports, the castle was not patronized by the fashionable or the wealthy, but by crowds who took advantage of its access by trolley. On summer Sundays, the open trolleys were packed. The castle had a few successful seasons, but as vacation and outing habits changed, its popularity declined and it closed. In 1914, it reopened for one last attempt, but this ended in disaster. The wooden structure and the stairs in the tower burned to the ground in the fall of 1914, so the tower which stands is truly a monument to the end of an era.

Courtesy of the B. H. Bartol Library

GREAT DEBATE

Oldest Wooden House?

Some historians consider the Fairbanks House in Dedham, Massachusetts, to be the oldest wooden frame house in America. Said to have been built by Jonathan Fairbank in 1636, the saltbox house measures seventy-five feet. Oak from England was reportedly used for the wooden structure. The roof, carrying a steep pitch, was originally designed for thatch, but town ordinances prevented the making of thatch roofs due to the fire hazard they created. Instead, a shingled roof was fashioned atop the homestead. Additions were made to accommodate the growing family and subsequent generations of Fairbanks continued to live in this historic dwelling until 1903.

Also claiming to be the oldest wooden house in America, this one with a written record to prove it, is the Balch House in Beverly, Massachusetts, built in 1636. After receiving one of the first recorded grants of land, John Balch and four others built houses for their families. Balch's house is the only one remaining from this settlement.

Also a wooden frame house, the original north portion is considered the oldest section of the structure, but since that time, many changes have been made, and the present structure is far from the original design, although the northern section still has its original timbers, summer beam, posts, and rafters.

We invite you to dicker over which house can truly be called the "oldest wooden frame house" in these parts. In our minds it is a toss up!

Oldest Stone House

According to authorities, the Henry Whitfield House in Guilford, Connecticut, built in 1639, is the oldest stone dwelling in New England. Originally it was the home of the Reverend Henry Whitfield, who led a group of Puritans from England and founded Guilford, Connecticut. When first built, it served as a church and meeting hall for the early settlers.

Oldest House on Cape Cod

In the center of historic Sandwich, in its original location, rests the Hoxie House, the oldest house on Cape Cod. A wooden frame house, many historians of the town say it was built in 1637. But the often mentioned "chimney brick bearing the date 1637" is not to be found.

Oldest House in Same Family

The Davis Homestead in Stonington, Connecticut, has been the center of the universe for the Davis family for 200 years. It is a fine record holder as the oldest house in New England to be owned by the same family. Under this ownership since 1772, the homestead has seen few changes in the patterns of daily life, and minimal changes in the farm itself.

Oldest Rebuilt House in Same Family

George Little came to Newbury, Massachusetts, from London, England, in 1640. A tailor by trade, he quickly turned to farming after acquiring an ample supply of land. His property has remained in the hands of his descendents to this day, more than 300 years later, and to our minds, this makes his house the oldest rebuilt house in the same family. (To explain "rebuilt:" the original farm house was built near a good spring but was moved to the present location in 1680. The house standing today was built in 1880, using part of the old house for its back. Enough of the first house went into the present house to justify our record, but we wanted you to know that it isn't exactly the same house George built way back when.)

Last House to Hear Pilgrims

The last house left standing in Plymouth, Massachusetts, where Pilgrims actually lived is the Howland House. A sign posted in front of the house confirms it as "The last house left in Plymouth whose walls had heard the voices of *Mayflower* Pilgrims." The older part of the house was built in 1666 by Jacob Mitchell who later sold the property to Jabez Howland in 1667. The house was occupied as a dwelling until 1912.

CHRIS MAYNARD

First Round Barn

The earliest and perhaps the best known circular barn is the Shaker barn at Hancock, Massachusetts, which dates back to 1826 and is owned today by the Hancock Shaker Village. The ninety-foot-diameter building made from fieldstones gathered from the nearby farmlands and foothills is an imposing structure. From the outside, the three-foot-thick limestone and granite walls resemble an impregnable fortress. Inside, the split-beam chestnut wood roof rafters converge like the spokes of a giant wagon wheel. And over the peaked roof, an eight-sided ventilating cupola surveys the surrounding Berkshire farmlands from a height of fifty feet.

According to architectural historians, the Hancock Shaker barn was the first circular barn to be built in America, and the only such barn whose walls are entirely stone. The Shakers selected this design because it eliminated a significant portion of heavy manual work in the care and feeding of the "fifty-two horned cattle and span of horses (working pair)" for which it was intended. It also permitted the Shaker farmers to go about their work without getting in each other's way. The cattle were kept in fifty-two pie-shaped stalls arranged in a circle on the ground floor. Each animal faced the center of the barn and was secured by two upright stanchions, allowing all to be fed from a common central mow. Directly above the animals was a second-floor circular wagon way made accessible by an outside inclined ramp, along which hay-filled wagons could pass two abreast and deposit their loads into the mow below.

The barn's design in some measure reflects the Shaker tradition of uniting religion with their daily lives and work. Shakers had always valued the circle as a practical and harmonious design. The barn gained a wide-spread reputation as a New England architectural rarity. Nathaniel Hawthorne and Herman Melville made special trips to see it in 1850 and Melville supposedly penned the comment "amazing" next to the paragraph in his guide book describing the great circular barn.

Courtesy of Peter Benes

Most Paneled Colonial House

Hunter House in Newport, Rhode Island, headquarters during the American Revolution for Admiral De Ternay of the French fleet, is the only colonial-built dwelling in New England in which all the rooms on the first and second floors are paneled from floor to ceiling. Built in 1748 from the plans of Peter Harrison, it is rated as one of the ten best examples of colonial residential architecture.

Most Old Houses in One Town

Ipswich, Massachusetts, has more First Period houses (those built prior to 1720) than any other town in America. A recent study reported that there were fifty-eight historic homes in this category still standing in Ipswich.

Most Stone Dwellings

Windsor County, Vermont, claims to have more stone buildings than any other county in New England. Churches and houses of note can be found in Chester, Cavendish, Reading, Baltimore, Plymouth, Springfield, and Weathersfield.

Most Historic 7/10's of a Mile

Great Road, which runs through and includes a portion of the old town of Smithfield or Lincoln, Rhode Island, forms New England's most historic 7/10's of a mile. Originally an Indian trail following close to North Woods and the Lime Rock District, the road in entirety once cut a path from Providence to Worcester. Many taverns were built along this main-traveled roadway. The Old Stone Chimney House, also called the Splendid Mansion, built by Eleazor Arnold in 1687, was one of the first buildings on Great Road. Despite many changes, this is one of the best preserved seventeenth-century houses in Rhode Island. Eleazor Arnold received his tavern license in 1710 and built seven homes along Great Road, one for each of his seven children. All but one is within the 7/10's of a mile mentioned above. Not far from Arnold Tavern is the Moffett Mill, a frame building with a stone foundation, constructed about 1812 and several other mills with unique architectural features.

Courtesy of Virginia L. Doris

Only House to Remember Jones

Appropriately named, the John Paul Jones House on Middle and State streets in Portsmouth, New Hampshire, is the only surviving structure in New England with which Jones had any documented associations. History shows that the famed naval hero occupied a room in the house between 1781 and 1782.

Only House Turned For Spite

About half a mile south of the quiet, tree-shaded common of Petersham, Massachusetts, at the intersection of Routes 32 and 122, stands a two-story white clapboard house that is the only such house ever turned around for spite.

The house was built by John Stowell in 1790, and it did face the northeast, toward the principal road and generally toward town, as proper houses should. Thus it remained for seventy-five years, until it was inherited by Forester Goddard, just over 100 years ago. In 1886, Goddard was employed by the town to repair and rebuild the west wall of the village cemetery — a retaining wall that still stands, as strong and sturdy as when he fashioned it over ninety years ago. He did a good job, but it did cost more than the town fathers had anticipated, and they refused to pay for it. Goddard argued his case, but to no avail. He never did collect what he thought was right, but Goddard was ingenious and he "took it out on the town" in his own unique fashion. "With no other help than what his wife could give him," as the town historian has chronicled, Goddard proceeded methodically and carefully to jack up his twenty-seven by forty-foot house, put croquet balls under it in the proper places, and slowly but surely inch it around until it faced south, toward the fields that he loved and with the back side to the town he despised.

And so this house remains today, nearly a century later. Forester Goddard is long since gone, but his house still stands with its back to the town — his supreme gesture of contempt for a place that would not pay an honest workman his due for a job well done.

Courtesy of Elmore B. Lyford

Only Octagonal House (of its kind)

Although there are several octagonal houses in New England, the one in West Gardiner, Maine, built about 1885 by Jesse Tucker, is unique in that its outer walls are constructed of ten-inch-wide slabs, about an inch thick, piled one above the other, flat side to flat side, for the whole three-story height of the building. Two-inch by four-inch boards are the standard dimensions.

Only Paper House

New England's only paper house is located at Pigeon Cove in Rockport, Massachusetts. Built by Elis F. Stenman in the 1950 s, furnishings include a desk and chair made out of the newspaper records of Colonel Lindburgh's flights and a piano constructed of newspapers accounting the expeditions of Admiral Peary. Not only is the furniture fireproof, but the papers are preserved for historical purposes. They can be unrolled and read.

Only Revolving House

Old time residents of Olmstead Hill sigh a little at the streams of sightseers, especially on weekends. The Foster's getaway place in the sky has given this sleepy old 1700 town, without a history of its own, its first tourist attraction — New England's only revolving house. The house turns on three different objects: a ball bearing fourteen feet in diameter, weighing three tons; the central steel axis that the spiral stair climbs around; and the one-and-a-half horsepower motor that uses as much current as a refrigerator are what keep the house rotating at a comfortable speed to provide a constantly changing view for its inhabitants. Ellie and Dick Foster came to this unique approach to living after falling in love with the piece of land that the house presently sits upon. The view includes hills, a pond, open meadow, and a spectacular forest, and they solved the problem of where to put the living room by giving all the rooms a fair chance to look out upon a different scene each day.

NEW YORK TIMES

First Full-Scale Solar House

The first complete, full-scale, suburban, sun-heated house stands in Lexington, Massachusetts. Built in 1949, it was the result of twenty years of solar energy research at MIT. The most striking feature of the house is its solar collector, the equipment which traps the sun's energy for heating use. This collector consists of 640 square feet of glass, two layers thick, over a similar area of thin (.025 inch) aluminum painted a heat absorbing black. While the aluminum sheet absorbs the solar energy, the glass serves the same purpose it does in a greenhouse. The sunshine is let in, but the longer waves of heat energy are kept from passing right out again. The energy in the sunshine is trapped and stored for use.

Highest Permanent Residence

With the Presidential Range of New Hampshire in his eastern windows and the Rosebrooks, Mt. Garfield, and Mt. Lafayette to the south and west, Nicholas Howe's home in Franconia, New Hampshire, elevated at 2,424 feet, is the highest permanent residence that we could find in New England.

First Covered Bridge House

A native of Webster, New Hampshire, set up housekeeping in a covered bridge, and established a record as being the first person in New England to make a home out of a covered bridge. The Webster bridge-house once spanned the Blackwater River at Swett's Mills. It was condemned for traffic in 1909, thereby reverting to the Pearson family which had owned it originally. Miss Jessie Pearson hired men and teams to haul the old structure to a hilltop a mile away, and remodeled it as a summer cottage. She added a fieldstone fireplace and chimney against one side, framed and boarded the open portals, and added a horizontal partition to make a second story for sleeping quarters

Courtesy of Dan Ford

Most Covered Bridges

New Hampshire claims to have more covered bridges than any other state in New England.

Shortest Covered Bridge

Prentiss Bridge in Langdon, New Hampshire, is the shortest covered bridge in the United States not on private property. It extends for thirty-six feet.

Longest Covered Bridge

Spanning the Connecticut River between Cornish, New Hampshire, and Windsor, Vermont, the Cornish-Windsor Bridge is the longest covered bridge in the United States. Originally built as an open bridge in 1796, the structure has been destroyed and rebuilt three times; the present structure, 460 feet long, was built in 1866.

Maine's Longest Covered Bridge

The old Morse Covered Bridge in Bangor, Maine, was painstakingly moved from its original site on Valley Avenue to a new resting place spanning the Kenduskeag Stream. The bridge is Maine's longest covered bridge, 212 feet.

Longest Covered Railroad Bridge

New England's longest covered railroad bridge was built in 1898, and spans the Missisquoi River at Swanton, Vermont. It stretches 369 feet.

Longest Wooden Bridge

On May 14, 1902, the "Mile Long Bridge" was officially opened to the public at Hampton Beach, New Hampshire. It took nearly a year to build, rested on 3,380 oak pilings, was 4,621 feet long and thirty feet wide. Records at the time indicate that it was the longest such bridge in the world. By 1930, the wood was showing signs of age, and in 1949, the wooden relic was dismantled.

Courtesy of John Holman

First Bridge Across Connecticut

In 1875, Colonel Enoch Hale built the first bridge across the Connecticut River. Known as the Tucker Bridge, it spanned the river between Walpole, New Hampshire, and Bellows Falls, Vermont.

Widest Bridge

The Crawford Street Bridge in Providence, Rhode Island, is the world's widest bridge. It spans 1,147 feet of the Providence River, connecting the downtown area with the East Side.

VERMONT DEVELOPMENT DEPARTMENT

Only Floating Bridge

The only floating bridge that we have discovered in New England spans a pond off Route 12, between Randolph and Northfield, Vermont, in the town of Brookfield. The present bridge was constructed in 1936, and is very safe, according to a local Vermonter who assures wary visitors: "The bridge ain't a mite dangerous," he says. "Haven't lost over a dozen cars in the pond all year."

Maine's Oldest Wire Bridge

Maine's oldest wire suspension bridge was completed in 1842 in New Portland. Hanging above the Carrabassett River, the bridge is approximately 185 feet long.

Largest Water Wheel

Elbert C. Aldrich's water wheel in Granby, Massachusetts, is the largest water wheel in New England. A hand-crafted wheel beside a historic grist mill, the overshot wheel is powered from nearby twenty-five-foot high falls. This wheel was constructed to commemorate the 100th anniversary of Aldrich's grandfather's settlement of the property. Made entirely of native white pine for long wear, its massive hub is twenty-eight inches in diameter and the circumference totals approximately eighty-three feet. The overall diameter is four feet larger than Henry Ford's similar water wheel in Sudbury, Massachusetts.

Only Wind-Powered Tool Mill

As far as we can tell, the wind-powered tool mill which Henry Glover built in West Dedham, Massachusetts, in 1890, was the only building of its kind in the state, and may well have been the last remaining such mill in all of New England. History has not recorded the day the mill blew down.

First American Architect

Peter Harrison, the architect in colonial America who designed the Redwood Library, Touro Synagogue, and Brick Market in Newport, King's Chapel in Boston, and Christ's Church in Cambridge, was the foremost architect of his time, and has been called the first American architect. Without formal training, he practiced architecture without pay as a gentlemanly pursuit. Originally from York, England, Harrison was also a farmer and trader in molasses, wine, rum, and mahogany for most of his life.

Biggest Architectural Letdown

An old, round, arched, stone structure in Newport, Rhode Island, is known to the locals as "The Old Stone Mill." For years, many Newporters and some experts believed the theory that the old mill was built by ancient Norsemen. If this had been the case, then Newport could have laid claim to having the oldest building in America. Unfortunately, in 1949, a young archaeologist under the auspices of the Newport Preservation Society did some digging around the base of the structure and found numerous colonial artifacts dating the mill to that period. His findings were a great disappointment to New Englanders dreaming of Vikings, and other records.

First Shopping Center

The Arcade Building in downtown Providence, Rhode Island, opened for business in 1829, and deserves acclaim as America's first shopping center. From the first excavation in 1827, to completion in 1829, the building cost Cyrus Butler, and the Providence Arcade Realty Company about $140,000. This was four years before Providence was even incorporated as a city, when its population was only 14,000. When the Arcade opened for business in 1829, a magazine praised it highly, calling it a "most truly splendid Bazar"; but had to add with gloom, "We sincerely hope that the gentlemen . . . will find the money, thus expended, at least a moderately profitable investment."

It turned out to be a quick success commercially, as well as the pride of the city. But after the peak of the Greek Revival, the Arcade's popularity (as architecture) went into decline. The building was renovated in 1901 after a fire did considerable damage to the ground floor. In 1944, a Providence utilities firm bought the building from the old Arcade Realty Company. The new owners threatened to tear it down but a group spearheaded by a covey of influential Providence business men preserved it.

Arcade business got a boost in 1968, when the building was given a new lighting system, modernized shopfronts, and an elevator. The last-mentioned item was a necessity: America in 1968 was a lot softer than in 1828, and the shops on the second and third floors were losing their business because no one wanted to climb all those stairs.

Courtesy of Ira Dember

First Automated Post Office

Rhode Island's main Providence Post Office was dedicated on October 20, 1960, and became the first fully automated post office in the country. It is 420 feet long, 300 feet wide, and has a parabolic, or clam-shell type roof of ten white, smoothly sloping contours supported by only two interior columns. Its 126,000 square feet of interior floor space, broken only by these two columns, makes possible the most efficient arrangement of mail processing equipment.

Tallest Control Tower

The tower at Logan Airport in Boston is the world's tallest control tower, rising twenty-two stories.

Closest City Airport

Logan Airport is only two miles from downtown Boston, making it a world record holder as the city airport that is closest to its city. Whether it is the most accessible airport in the world is yet another matter!

First Skyscraper

Prudential Center in Boston was the first skyscraper in New England. Built on land that was once declared a "blighted open area," this thirty-two-acre site, formerly the switching yard for the Boston and Albany Railroad and the location for the Old Mechanic Building, now houses twelve modern constructions. Standing fifty-two stories, the Prudential Center Tower measures 750 feet in height. The rectangular tower is 150 feet wide and 178 feet long, and contains about 1 million square feet of useable office floor space. It is surrounded by a twenty-five foot-wide moat, filled year round with 225,000 gallons of heated water eighteen inches deep. The moat is lined with aluminum and 1,125,000 deep blue ceramic tiles, and it is crossed by four twenty-five-foot concrete bridges, one on each of the tower's sides. The 10,000 windows in the building are sealed in place with 2 million separate fasteners and the ten acres of glass windows are cleaned by a forty-foot-long window washing gondola suspended from the open fifty-first floor.

Tallest Building

The John Hancock building in Boston is the tallest building in New England, rising to a height of 790 feet. And its observatory, at 740 feet, is the highest man-made vantage point in the region.